Students explore the varying needs, interests, and capabilities of adult learning—how adults learn and how classroom climate and teacher attitudes can facilitate or hinder learning. Students review the entire curriculum development process and the steps in instructional design as these pertain to teaching adults. The authors help students bridge the gap between theory and practice by suggesting ideas and materials to help develop effective teaching styles.

The authors stress the importance of using community resources in the adult classroom. Adult students need practical day-to-day information in such areas as job opportunities, health, money management, legal rights, and child care. They need to know what resources are available to them in their community and how to access these community agencies. **ADULTS TEACHING ADULTS** discusses the use of the local community services directory as a classroom resource. Specific suggestions are presented for classroom activities, such as panel discussions and interviews involving social agency representatives and community leaders. The authors also recommend involving students in agency visits, role plays, media productions, and evaluation efforts as part of their learning experiences.

ADULTS TEACHING ADULTS offers practical suggestions geared to the realities of the adult classroom. The book addresses the working concerns of adult educators, part-time teachers, and students who wish to explore the opportunities available in the field of adult education.

Adults Teaching Adults

Principles and Strategies

John R. Verduin, Jr.
Harry G. Miller
Charles E. Greer

LEARNING CONCEPTS, AUSTIN, TEXAS

Library of Congress Cataloging in Publication Data

Verduin, John R.
  Adults teaching adults.

  Includes bibliographies and index.
  1. Adult education.   2. Peer-groups tutoring of
students.   I. Miller, Harry G., 1941-   joint author.
II. Greer, Charles E., 1926-   joint author.   III. Title.
LC5219.V46   374   77-9259
ISBN 0-89384-015-7

Learning Concepts
2501 N. Lamar
Austin, Texas 78705

Edited by Linda Schexnaydre

To
All Adult Educators

and

Janet, John, Susan, Mary, Alicia, Michael, Anne,
Deirdre and Phyllis

CONTENTS

Preface   xi

Part I   Introduction to Adult Education Instruction

1. Adult Education Instruction: An Introduction   3

   Adult Education—Complex and Dynamic   3
   Diversity of Adult Education Efforts   4
   Variety of Teachers Involved   6
   Improvement of Adult Instruction   7

Part II   Foundations for Adult Learning

2. Overview of Learning for Adults: A Perceptual
   Approach   9

   Individual Behavior   9
   Implications for Teaching/Learning   12
   General Instructional Strategies   15
   Three Domains of Behavior   16
   Selected Bibliography   19

3. Curriculum Model for Adult Education   21

   Goals   22
   Instruction   24
   Evaluation   24
   Rationale   28
   Outside Political Forces   28
   Selected Bibliography   33

4. Bases for General Goals in Adult Education   35

   Philosophical Base   35
   Historical Base   36
   Legislative Base   40
   Selected Bibliography   47

Part III   Instructional Processes and Procedures

5. Model for Adult Instruction   49

    Overview of the Model   49
    Assessing Entering Behavior and Specifying
        Objectives   52
    Designing Learning Units and Procedures   61
    Presenting Learning Units and Creating a Learning
        Climate   63
    Adult Performance, Feedback, and Assessment   64
    Selected Bibliography   65

6. Specifying Objectives for Adult Instruction   67

    Use of Objectives   67
    Levels of Objectives   68
    Selection of Objectives   71
    Behavioral Objectives   73
    Selected Bibliography   79

7. Organizing Adult Instructional Plans   81

    Instructional Plan   82
    Constructing Instructional Plans   91
        Instructional Plan on Measuring the
            Length of Steel Pipe for Installation   93
        Instructional Plan on Nationhood for an
            Adult Basic Education Program   96
    Selected Learning Activities   102
        Crossword Puzzle   102
        Wordsearch Puzzle   105
        Word Scramble Puzzle   108
        Cryptogram Puzzle   110
        Missing Letter Search   111
        Rank-Order Technique   113
        Extrapolation Technique   116

Differential Technique   118
Should/Should Not—Is/Is Not Technique   119
Preparation Reminders   121
Selected Bibliography   123

8. Methods for Adult Instruction   125

Explanation Techniques   126
Demonstrations   128
Questioning Techniques   130
Drill   135
Tutoring   139
Inquiry   143
Small Groups   145
Selected Bibliography   151

9. Evaluation in Adult Instruction   153

Meanings of Evaluation   153
Program and Institution Evaluation—General
    Level   155
Evaluation for Courses and Instructional Plans—
    Intermediate and Specific Levels   157
Constructing Objective Test Items   158
    Multiple-Choice   159
    Matching   160
    True-False   162
    Completion   163
Constructing Essay Test Items   164
Constructing Performance Test Items   165
    Checklists   166
    Rating Scales   168
    Anecdotal Records   171
Determining Achievement Levels   173
Selected Bibliography   175

Part IV   Selected Ideas for the Adult Instructor

10. Community Services and Instruction   177

        Community Services Directory   178
           Content of the Directory   178
           Preparation of the Directory   181
        Using the Directory in the Classroom   183
        Selected Bibliography   189

11. Competency-Based Instruction for Adults   191

        Strenghts   193
        Potential Shortcomings   195
        Selected Bibliography   199

    Index   201

LIST OF FIGURES

3.1 Goals 23

3.2 Instruction 24

3.3 Evaluation 26

34. Curriculum Design 27

3.5 General Curriculum Model 31

5.1 Adult Instructional Model 51

5.2 Psychomotor Categories 60

6.1 Levels of Objectives 69

8.1 Student Achievement Record 142

8.2 Brainstorming Group 146

8.3 Discussion Group 147

8.4 Tutorial Group 148

PREFACE

The education of adults is a diverse and complex process affecting many people from all walks of life. The diversity is seen not only in the kinds of programs, courses, and priorities in adult education, but also in the kinds of people who provide the instruction for adults. Instructors represent a wide range of teaching and non-teaching backgrounds and differ in their training and experiences. Since the key to instructional success rests with adult teachers, it is imperative that teachers perform at the most effective level possible.

Considerable theory, knowledge, and practical ideas exist which can assist adult teachers in improving their professional behavior in the classroom. Various models, constructs, strategies, and techniques are available which make the instructional process more effective and, in turn, insure greater learning for adult students. This text attempts to provide both the theoretical constructs and the practical applications so that adult teachers can see reasons for various instructional strategies and can learn techniques for implementing them.

This book is designed as an introductory text to assist the active practitioner—both teacher and administrator—in working with adults. Further, it should help college students in their preparation for a career in adult education. Finally, it may assist the theoretician in developing curricula for implementation and testing, in designing some instructional packages for use in classrooms, or in providing constructs for needed research.

Part I serves as an introduction to adult education instruction by showing the complexity and diversity of adult education programs, students, and teachers. It further suggests that teaching adults is complex and that improved behavior on the part of teachers is necessary to do this job.

Part II offers an overview of adult behavior and learning and provides an analysis of the philosophical, historical, and legislative bases for goal setting in adult education programs. The curriculum development model will prepare teachers to participate in the numerous curriculum development activities currently taking place in the field of adult education.

Part III gives special attention to the instructional processes and procedures the adult instructor may utilize in teaching and in learning situations with adult students. Chapters in this part focus on an instructional model with various elements, on the very important process of selecting and specifying objectives or goals for adult instruction, on the task of organizing instructional plans for adult students, on the all-important methods and strategies of instructing adults, and on the critical area of evaluation of instruction. Theoretical and practical considerations are given throughout this entire section of the book.

Part IV presents selected ideas for the adult instructor. The use of various community resources in adult instruction is discussed in Chapter Nine. These can be a beneficial resource to adults, particularly to the undereducated and the underemployed, and a significant tool for teaching and learning in an adult classroom. The final chapter takes a critical look at competency-based instruction for adults which has emerged as a result of the Adult Performance Level Study conducted at the University of Texas. The chapter offers some ideas on use and some cautions when dealing with competency- or performance-based instruction in adult education programs.

We have appreciated the encouragement, advise, and criticism from practicing adult educators at the local, state, and national levels during the preparation of this text. Salient comments came from those who practice adult education in correctional facilities, Adult Basic Education centers, adult vocational centers, sheltered workshops, state departments of education, and other locations where adult education is of great import. To list all of them would be a never-ending process; however, their constructive comments and encouragement are most appreciated.

We would also like to thank Karen Hunt, Ann Croessman, and Jill Vaughn for their invaluable assistance in getting this manuscript ready for publication.

The use of this text by practicing and future adult educators should bring more precision to their professional abilities in teaching and associated instructional activities. With more precision in professional behavior, better learning goals for adults can be achieved. It is the hope of the three of us that these better learning goals will be realized in adult education.

John R. Verduin, Jr.
Harry G. Miller
Charles E. Greer

Adults Teaching Adults

1

Adult
Education Instruction:
An Introduction

ADULT EDUCATION — COMPLEX AND DYNAMIC

The education of adults is a multifaceted, complex process which encompasses many subject and interest areas. It is as broad and varied as those it serves. It encompasses Adult Basic Education (teaching basic learning and survival skills to the under-educated), continuing education efforts for personal and professional growth, and enrichment activities for the highly educated. It is designed for personal skill development, for enhanced career opportunities, or for enjoyment. It can involve a very short duration of time or several years of effort. Finally, it serves a diversity of students and includes a varied population of adult teachers.

The scope and role of adult education has increased significantly in the last generation. The adult educator is found in virtually every area of the nation. Programs geared to the vocationally ambitious, the unskilled, the curious, and to those who desire a fulfilling leisure are all provided. Several trends account for the continuing growth of a movement that will one day provide a system of lifelong education to every citizen.

The continual growth of a sophisticated technology is one factor that promotes adult education. Technology requires a highly skilled labor force. For those who failed to acquire such skills in their previous educational efforts, adult education provides a means by which they may enhance their capabilities.

Many Americans did not experience success during their public school tenure and did not acquire basic academic skills and the terminal diploma. Without these skills and the high school diploma, adults are finding it very difficult to function in society. As a result, Adult Basic Education constitutes a large portion of adult education efforts today.

The rapid rate of change in society also creates a demand for the adult educator. Rapid change has become a characteristic of modern society. It forces many to face the unhappy prospect of vocational obsolescence and the need for retraining. Others are bewildered by a rapidly changing environment. For them adult education provides a means by which they can inform themselves and thus become better and more productive citizens.

Affluence, abundance, and the leisure that these provide combine to support the continued growth of adult education. People now spend countless hours away from the world of work. Many are also faced with the four-day work week, an increase in life expectancy, and early retirement. Adult education programs can facilitate the constructive use of leisure.

DIVERSITY OF ADULT EDUCATION EFFORTS

Adult education itself has developed a broad and varied base of institutional sponsorship. Lacking the simple symbolism and the distinctive identity of the public school and the college campus, adult education programs take place primarily in institutions organized for other purposes. Although adult education is a concern of most colleges, universities, and elementary and secondary schools, it is not exclusively the domain of public education.

Adult education activities take place in such "non-educational" institutions as museums, libraries, social agencies, voluntary associations, YMCAs, churches, industrial organizations, labor unions, professional societies, and governmental agencies at all levels. Fewer in number are those institutions created primarily for the education of adults, such as proprietary schools, independent and public adult education centers, and the agricultural extension service. In fact, adult education and its many program efforts can occur in various forms and institutions. Some examples follow.

1. *Sheltered workshops*—Sheltered workshops are generally nonprofit public institutions which provide rehabilitating activity for physically, emotionally, and mentally handicapped adults who have the potential for some level of competitive employment. Frequently, such workshops provide for vocational capability testing and specialized training for clients attending the programs.

2. *Community colleges*—Community colleges are generally two-year, postsecondary institutions which provide Adult Basic Education programs, academic programs, vocational programs, and adult self-enrichment courses for a specific geographic region.

3. *Adult Basic Education centers*—The Adult Basic Education center offers an instructional program for adults who need basic reading, writing, and arithmetic skills to function adequately as self-sufficient members of society. Further, coursework is usually offered to help the adult student successfully pass the General Educational Development (GED) test and receive a high school equivalency certificate.

4. *Cooperative extension centers*—Cooperative extension centers, headquartered in state land-grant colleges, provide assistance in agriculture and home economics and coordinate efforts in these areas by federal, state, and county governments. In addition, programs have also included health, community development, conservation, and public affairs. Programs and

services associated with cooperative extension education are generally nonclassroom, nongraded, and noncredit.

5. *Adult vocational and technical schools*—These are institutions organized for the purpose of training the adult in one or more semiskilled, skilled, or technical occupations. Frequently, such schools operate and function within the jurisdiction of a school district under a board of education.

6. *YMCA/YWCA centers*—These institutions offer varied enrichment and recreational courses ranging from beginning swimming to Chinese cooking. Some centers may also offer basic education classes.

7. *Community education centers*—Community education is a coordinated effort to meet the mutual educational needs of the individuals and groups of a particular community.

8. *Evening program centers*—Evening-oriented programs can be offered in a variety of institutions, both public and private, but generally the programs occur in a public school building. The programs and courses are offered at hours other than those commonly used for elementary and secondary school classes for persons not engaged in full-time schooling. Typically, offerings include self-enrichment courses, vocational training, vocational and recreational activities, and Adult Basic Education. Such offerings are not necessarily provided in only one facility but are housed in a variety of locations for the most direct and convenient program delivery possible.

VARIETY OF TEACHERS INVOLVED

Besides the obvious variety shown in adult education centers, programs, and content areas, there is considerable variety in the instructors involved. Teachers generally are hired on a part-time basis. They may hold college degrees in teaching, but many do not. They may have considerble training and experience in their teaching areas or possess very little of either. It is not uncommon to have individuals who are not professional educators in such adult education classes as welding, nursing, flower arranging, and cooking. It is also not uncommon to have professionally trained adult teachers instructing in areas other than their original areas of formal study; for example, a high school English teacher involved in basic reading instruction, social studies teachers working in GED areas, and science teachers teaching math to the undereducated.

This great variation in adult teachers, their preparation and training, can be explained. First, few undergraduate programs exist for the preparation of adult teachers in the many curriculum areas involved, whereas training programs exist for the preparation of early childhood teachers, science teachers, and special education teachers for public schools. Graduate programs at the master's and doctoral levels are being developed, however. Secondly, the diversity of programs and courses offered to adults requires people with varied expertise and interests, regardless of formal educational background. The auto mechanic or registered nurse will probably have little formal training in teaching techniques, but their knowledge base on the subject matter is sound. Finally, the lack of a formal place in the educational system for adult education has prevented the focus on training and preparation of certified personnel. In any case the variety of adult teachers found in this field of endeavor is healthy, particularly if these teachers can enhance their behavior to become more effective.

IMPROVEMENT OF ADULT INSTRUCTION

Adult instruction refers to a teacher's interaction with adults as a means of influencing their behavior. Teaching strategies direct adults to specific tasks and experiences so that learning will result from these encounters. Adult instruction should not be a haphazard effort but should be designed to be specific and directed toward learning goals. Given this rationale, teachers of adults need to be as effective, expedient, and accurate in their instruction as possible.

Teaching involves making a variety of decisions in a variety of situations in the classroom. Because of this it appears necessary that adult teachers be given various models to help them analyze situations in a classroom so that they can make better decisions as they influence adult students toward certain selected goals. With systems or models the adult teacher can understand the nature of the adult learning situation and then can strive for more precise behavior as he or she carries out the various pedagogical moves in a classroom. For example, adult teachers typically ask students a number of questions in a classroom. Given a model or guide for assessing the level of cognition (thinking) resulting from their questions, teachers can then make decisions about their questioning style. Once aware that they may ask questions which require lower level cognitive responses, teachers may, if deemed necessary, move the level of student thought to a higher plane. With the help of models, constructs, and guides, this is very possible.

Teaching is a series of observable actions which can be reviewed, enhanced, altered, changed, and repeated. If instruction is to be more than chance, models for adult instruction, from which adult teachers may base their instructional efforts, must be designed and tested. An instruction model is a means for increasing understanding and control of teaching for better learning. It is an ordering of teaching effort which provides a logic for actions. Instructional recipes are not enough for adult education situations since every adult student, adult classroom, and adult purpose are different. Instructors need basic principles to guide them in selecting particular methods that will assist the adult learner in his or her specific situation. To help the adult instructor make better decisions and move to more effective instruction, a variety of theoretical and practical ideas are presented in this text.

2

Overview of Learning
for Adults:
A Perceptual Approach

The educator's basic job is to bring about some new and desired student behavior. Teachers, in essence, design and carry out the instructional experience so that students can gain a new behavior, practice it if necessary, and learn when to use it in an applied situation. Behavior, therefore, is the key consideration for adult educators as they carry out their professional duties, and learning (changing behavior) is the primary focus of the instructional act.

INDIVIDUAL BEHAVIOR

Human behavior is a very broad and complex phenomenon, involving numerous components. It is also a very individualized phenomenon; each person possesses a different "package" of experiences, values, needs, goals, persuasions, and ideas which cause one individual to behave differently (even if only slightly) from another individual. Since the task of education is to change behavior, it is imperative that these many differences be examined and considered by the adult educator as he designs a learning experience.

One view of learning and behavior change which holds strong meaning for adult education is the perceptual theory of psychology (ASCD, 1959; Combs & Snygg, 1959). This theory suggests that how an individual views (perceives) people, objects, and events in his environment will have much to do with how he behaves. For example, if an adult perceives the need to learn a new mechanical operation, he will be motivated toward learning it. If he sees the values derived from learning to become a carpenter, chances are good he will strive to learn the appropriate behaviors of a carpenter. If he believes that arriving at work on time has its rewards, he will be there. The perceptions of various objects and events in the environment can have a strong impact on the total behavior of an individual; and, of course, perceiving things differently will cause people to behave differently. If a teacher wishes to change the behavior of an individual toward some desired new behavior, he must modify the way the individual views (perceives) his particular part of the world.

Because of the significance of people's perceptions for behavior and learning, it is most important to give careful consideration to those things that determine or affect human perception. There are several perceptual determinants; the identifiable ones are:

> *Beliefs*—What adults believe to be true affects their behavior; whether these take the form of faith, knowledge, assumption, or superstition, beliefs are reality to individuals, and they behave as if the beliefs were true.
>
> *Values*—People's feelings about what is important to them; this could be related to ideas, a way of life, material things, or people.
>
> *Needs*—What individuals require to maintain or enhance themselves. According to this theory, needs can be divided into two kinds:
> 1. Physiological needs, such as food, water, air, shelter
> 2. Social needs, such as need for approval and acceptance, status, prestige, power

Attitudes—An emotionalized belief about the worth (or lack of worth) of someone or something.

Self-experience (self-concept)—How people see themselves, how they feel about being that person, how they think others see them, how they see other people, and how they feel about this; their concept of the roles they play, how they feel about these, and their ideal role concepts.

Because adults have lived in the world for a given number of years, they have had the opportunity to gain many perceptions of their environment and all the objects and events in it. The sum total of all of these perceptions forms the past experiences of the individual. Adults' past experiences form their behavior as they begin the class and are the starting points from which the behavior change (learning) process must proceed. Adult behavior at this stage is probably much more rigid than that of younger children in school because it has been formed over longer periods of time.

Another concept in the perceptual theory of human behavior which has relevance to the adult educator is the general notion of threat. Threat is the perception of an imposed force requiring a change in behavior, values, or beliefs. One of the greatest threats to people is the requirement to change behavior when beliefs, values, or needs remain unchanged. People are most threatened when they are forced to change the ways in which they seek to maintain or enhance self-organization.

Threat in turn causes defensive behavior and a narrowing and constricting of the perceptual field. When threatened, people seek to maintain themselves, not grow or be enhanced. Imagination, initiative, and creativity can be destroyed as people tend to concentrate on the safe and secure. In the absence of threat, however, people can gain new perceptions; begin to review their personal attitudes, values, needs, and beliefs; and thus begin to form new and different behaviors. The openness to new ideas, therefore, is important in gaining new behaviors.

Psychologists suggest that people's perceptions and behaviors are not fixed. Change is not an easy process; but beliefs, values, needs, attitudes, and self-experiences can be modified. Past experiences remain the same, but the interpretation of them can be different. Each individual's behavior "package" was formed differently and may require different inputs and experiences for change to take place. With all of these ideas in mind, it is now appropriate to look at ways in which change in perception and behavior (learning) may take place.

IMPLICATIONS FOR TEACHING/LEARNING

An adult walks into a classroom for instruction with his own values, needs, beliefs, attitudes, self-concept, and past experiences. With this unique set he will be ready to learn things which affect his perceptual screen and which have personal meaning only to him. The motivation to learn something is present if the individual can see the personal meaning involved. If the goals for instruction are not those of the learner or not accepted as valid by the learner, the content will have little or no meaning for him. Unless he can see the personal meaning involved, it is doubtful if real learning (behavioral change) will occur in the adult student. This personal-meaning factor places the burden on the instructor to view the adult as he is and to look at the adult's world as the adult sees it. The instructor can more easily understand each student in his class if he tries to see the adult student and his world from the student's viewpoint. This understanding of the adult student and his world requires close, personal interaction between student and instructor.

Because of the uniqueness of each adult learner, the educative process must start with the important problems of the learners and the needs relevant to them. Maslow (1970) emphasizes personal needs strongly by suggesting that felt needs are the primary influences on an individual's behavior and that unsatisfied needs are the prime sources of motivation. He organizes all human needs into five needs systems and further states that the five needs are hierarchical in nature. Adults progress up the ladder only when they are secure with one need system. After having fulfilled one need, the adult can then be motivated to move to the next level. The five identified levels are (in ascending order):

Basic—Needs which reflect physiological and survival goals (shelter, clothing, food)

Safety—Needs of security, orderliness, protection (adequate salary, insurance policies, personal protection)

Belongingness—Needs for interpersonal relationships; feeling accepted, appreciated (family ties, friendships, group member-ships)

Ego-Status—Need for gaining status; ambition and desire to excel (various professional and social awards)

Self-Actualization—Need for personal growth, greater creativity, greater personal achievement (seeking autonomy, taking risks, seeking freedom to act)

To understand adults, their behaviors and goals, the adult educator must gain insight into the adult's unsatisfied needs. A careful assessment is required to determine where the adult is and what he deems important.

Since these needs as well as values and attitudes are such important determiners of human behavior, education must seek to help adult students know precisely what needs, values, and attitudes are important to them and how these relate to each other. This is particularly important to the adult who returns to a class-room for instruction. The instructor and other professional workers will have to assist the adult in clarifying his needs and values (which can be quite different from the instructor's) and help him set a realistic goal for such added instruction. The additional instruction, of whatever duration, must move the adult to his own goals, but these goals can be attained only if they are carefully discussed and realistically refined. Since success in attaining goals is important for the student, the goals must be, after clarification, those of the adult student. Learners really learn in response to their own needs and perceptions, not those of their teachers.

In addition, an open, supportive, and positive classroom

climate must be established to foster the appropriate behavioral change. Again, this has particular meaning to many adult students returning to a classroom for additional learning. The open, supportive classroom is necessary because the adult may perceive the school, classroom, and teacher as negative factors (a threat) because of past experiences in similar situations. If the adult left school because of personal difficulties or expulsion, his perception of the new situation will not be conducive to gaining new experiences. A positive classroom climate with the absence of threat will help to open the perceptual screen so that new learning can take place.

Since the modification of perception and behavior is very personal, the instructional program should be as individually based as possible. This is not an easy task because of the heterogenous nature of many adult classrooms. However, changing the behavior of each individual is a unique process and should be treated as such. Individual progress is especially critical for an adult learner; he must know that he is achieving, not wasting his time in a school situation. Keeping the individual moving toward his goals will do much to retain him in the learning situation; and since retention is a problem for many adult programs, progress must always be evident.

The lack of progress in achieving goals is tied closely to the low self-concept and lack of self-confidence that some adult learners possess. Many undereducated adults who have experienced little, if any, success in a school situation have probably acquired rather poor self-concepts. Observable progress toward meaningful goals, however, will cause change in the self-concept and result in different behaviors, particularly in the area of motivation for more learning.

Finally, since each individual is different and is exploring experiences which have personal meaning to him, adults must be given appropriate time and guidance to gain the new behavior. It must be kept in mind that individual differences include different rates of learning; some adults learn things more slowly than others. This is particularly true for those who possess low scholastic skills. However, with the exception of the severely handicapped, most adults can learn or accomplish tasks. The aptitude to learn something, therefore, is really a function of time. It takes more time for some adults to learn certain tasks and perhaps less to learn others. Thus, learning should again be individually based.

GENERAL INSTRUCTIONAL STRATEGIES

Although much of the remainder of this volume is devoted to instruction, some general implications of the perceptual theory in regard to instruction will be offered here, with more explication later.

Group work has been found effective for changing perceptions and behaviors in the areas of attitudes and beliefs. Within a democratically led group, the individual can retain beliefs and attitudes until he has had the opportunity to reexamine them carefully and can then change when he feels it necessary. The open and nonthreatening group will allow the individual to interact with others who possess different beliefs and attitudes and permit an interchange of ideas. This interchange of ideas is what causes the individual to rethink his position and then change.

Individual problem solving and personal investigation are also effective means for achieving significant behavior change in an individual. Within the framework of these procedures the person can pursue areas of personal meaning, seek out alternative solutions, and make the decision that seems appropriate. Personal meaning is involved, and change in behavior will be personal.

Activity learning, with hands-on experience, is an appropriate method of changing behavior. This may be of particular import for those persons in adult classes who possess low scholastic skills. Words in a book may bother an adult student, but activity learning would ease this process and bring about appropriate change.

Instructional activities should be task oriented and include active participation by the learner. Adults should experience success in completing the activity and should be able to demonstrate the skill in new situations. Finally, the instruction should be adult centered in an open, nonthreatening atmosphere with high priority on personal needs and interests. The instructors working closely and cooperatively with adults can be the key to significant behavior change.

The need for adults to see the achievement of what they have learned and for the instructor to respond to achievement with positive acknowledgment and praise is important. With achievement and success, a positive pattern of experiences is being developed which will help the student learn more difficult content. The cliche' that "nothing breeds success like success" is true for most adults. The more positive or healthy the perception of self, the more the person will be willing to venture and explore the new and unique. A positive self-concept provides a readiness which is a prerequisite for all learning.

THREE DOMAINS OF BEHAVIOR

Behavior may also be thought of as occurring in three major domains, which correspond directly to the three categories of educational objectives—cognitive, affective, and psychomotor. All three domains of behavior are important in the work of educators because each represents skills that an adult needs to function effectively. The *cognitive domain* represents a mental process—knowing and retaining information, making judgments or evaluations. One example is knowing how to use a thermometer accurately. For the cognitive domain, an adult's mastery of the behavior will not be apparent until some overt act is performed. In this example the adult will probably have to take a temperature in order to display that the knowledge is there.

The *psychomotor domain* involves the actual performance of some physical skill, such as soldering an electric appliance correctly.

The adult may know what the theory is behind some concept—repairing a carburetor, for example—but he may not have the physical (psychomotor) skill to put it into practice. A person's knowledge would therefore fall into the cognitive domain and not the psychomotor.

The *affective domain* pertains to behaviors involving attitudes or values, such as being at work on time. The adult student may "know" that consistently being on time is important; but if he does not do it, he is reflecting a poor attitude or actually expressing a lack of value for this particular matter. Again, the adult's possession of this affective state or behavior is evidenced only when he overtly displays it in a real situation. In this case the student has not internalized the appropriate behavior because there is no overt expression of it.

Although the adult education teacher is primarily concerned with the instructional activities in his immediate area, he should perhaps take a careful look at the broader picture of educational experiences that are defined and developed to assist the adult student in becoming a better functioning individual in a democratic society. This broad picture of educational experiences designed for adults is called the curriculum. With a knowledge of what the curriculum is, what it can and should do, and how it can be organized and developed, the adult educator can be more effective, not only in his teaching, but also in his developmental activities and general professional duties as a teacher.

SELECTED BIBLIOGRAPHY

Adult learning interests and experiences. In P. Cross, & J. Valley (Eds.), *Planning non-traditional programs: An analysis of the issues for post secondary education.* San Francisco: Jossey-Bass, 1974.

Association for Supervision and Curriculum Development. *Learning more about learning.* Washington, D.C.: Author, 1959.

Association for Supervision and Curriculum Development. *Freeing capacity to learn.* Washington, D.C.: Author, 1960.

Association for Supervision and Curriculum Development. *New dimensions in learning.* Washington, D.C.: Author, 1962.

Association for Supervision and Curriculum Development. *Perceiving, behaving, becoming: A new focus in education.* Washington, D.C.: Author, 1962.

Birren, J.E. (Ed.). *Handbook of aging and the individual.* Chicago: University of Chicago Press, 1959.

Bischof, L. J. *Adult psychology.* New York: Harper & Row, 1969.

Bloom, B. S., et al. *Taxonomy of educational objectives, the classification of educational goals, handbook I: Cognitive domain.* New York: David McKay Co., 1956.

Combs, A., & Snygg, D. *Individual behavior* (Rev. ed.). New York: Harper & Row, 1959.

Dickinson, G. *Teaching adults: A handbook for instructors.* Toronto: New Press, 1973.

Gagne, R. M. *The conditions of learning* (2nd ed.). New York: Holt, Rinehart, & Winston, 1970.

Kidd, J. R. *How adults learn* (Rev. ed.). New York: Association Press, 1973.

Knowles, M. S. *The modern practice of adult education.* New York: Association Press, 1970.

Knowles, M. S. *The adult learner: A neglected species.* Houston: Gulf Publishing Co., 1973.

Krathwohl, D. R., Bloom, B. S., & Masia, B. *Taxonomy of educational objectives, the classification of educational goals, handbook II: Affective domain.* New York: David McKay Co., 1964.

Kuhlen, R. G. (Ed.). *Psychological backgrounds of adult education.* Chicago: The Center for the Study of Liberal Education for Adults, 1963.

Lorge, I. *Psychology of adults.* Washington, D.C.: Adult Education Association of the U.S.A., 1963.

Lumsden, D. B., & Sherron, R. H. (Eds.). *Experimental studies in adult learning and memory.* Washington, D.C.: Hemisphere Publishing Co., 1975.

Maslow, A. H. *Motivation and personality* (2nd ed.). New York: Harper & Row, 1970.

Tough, A. M. *The adult's learning projects; a fresh approach to theory and practice in adult learning.* Toronto: Ontario Institute for Studies in Education, 1971.

3
Curriculum Model for Adult Education

The curriculum can be defined as all of the learning experiences that come under the auspices of a learning center, a school, or school district, whether these occur in a regular classroom, in a special laboratory (e.g., a machine shop), or outside of the school. This chapter provides a general curriculum structure or model to aid the adult educator as he develops and supervises both short-range and long-range experiences for his adult students. Since changing adult behavior takes time and numerous behaviors are needed for the adult to function fully in a democratic society, the adult educator must consider more than day-to-day instructional experiences. He must develop a consistent and coherent program for his students. He must work with other instructors to formulate a carefully defined program of learning for the adult student. The major curriculum elements must complement one another if the curriculum is to be suitable for preparing adults for successful living.

GOALS

The statement of curriculum goals or objectives focuses on what is important for adults to learn. This statement should answer the question: "What is worth learning in the adult's point of view?" The goals can be precisely those of the adult or cooperatively defined and refined by the adult learner and his instructors. The goals can even be suggested by a third party as long as the adult learner sees their personal meaning and is desirous of achieving them.

Goals may be stated at three different levels, corresponding to the different levels of curriculum development (Krathwohl, 1965). At the *general level,* long-term goals guide an entire program. For example, a general goal for an Adult Basic Education program might be that the students will be able to pass a General Educational Development (GED) test at the end of instruction. As a terminal goal for an adult vocational program, the goal might be that the adult will be able to secure an apprentice position in a given vocational field. Though quite general in nature, these goals serve as a referent for more specific instructional activities. Curriculum goals give the teacher of adults a general focus, as well as the flexibility and freedom to achieve these goals in a manner which best suits his students, his situation, and his own teaching style.

The *intermediate level* goal statement is designed for smaller units of instruction, such as a course, a semester of study, a unit of work, or even a year of instruction. The adult educator will, in conjunction with adults, specify goals for a unit on arc welding, a course on child care, or a year of typing. For example, the adult instructor can specify that at the end of a year of typing the adults will be able to type thirty words a minute with a maximum of two errors. For a child-care course, the adults in the class might be expected to list and carry out ten games appropriate to a certain age level of children. Goals at this level are quite precise, are stated in terms of needed behaviors, and can be expressed in the three major learning domains—cognitive, affective, and psychomotor.

Goals at the *specific level* focus on what can be achieved as a result of daily or short lessons with adult students. These statements are very precise and give the adult educator a very clear direction as to what behaviors the adult should display at the end of a day or two of instruction. For example, the student might be expected to list and describe briefly the three major branches of government. As the instructor develops specific instructional objectives, he must coordinate these with total program goals.

GOALS   (What is worth learning in the adult view?)

General level—General, abstract
statements to cover longer
periods of time (i.e., programs,
years of study)

Intermediate level—More precise
statements to cover more manageable packages of instruction
(i.e., unit, semester, module,
year)

Specific level—Very precise
statements to cover daily
and short-term experiences
(i.e., daily lesson, short
topics)

Statements
specified
in
cognitive,
affective,
and
psychomotor
domains

Figure 3.1—**Goals**

INSTRUCTION

Instruction is the delivery system through which the curriculum goals will be achieved. In designing the instructional activities and organizing the content to be taught, the adult teacher answers the question: "How will the goals be accomplished?" Instruction in this case is the interaction among the instructor, the adult student, and the content aimed at changing the behavior of the student. Since the next chapter is devoted to an instruction model and ensuing chapters focus primarily on the teaching process, little more will be said at this time. Note, however, the components of the instructional design model which follow and the relationship of instruction activities to the rest of the curriculum.

INSTRUCTION ACTIVITIES (How will the goals be accomplished?)

> Define terminal goals
> Assess entering behavior
> Define and organize content
> Select materials
> Invent and/or select strategies
> Create classroom climate
> Assess learning

Figure 3.2—**Instruction**

EVALUATION

A third major element in the curriculum structure is evaluation: "Were the goals accomplished?" This assessment process attempts to determine the extent that adult students have achieved the desired goals (new behaviors) as a result of the instructional process. Without this information, curriculum modification cannot take place, and adult progress cannot be monitored.

Evaluation procedures should be set up before instruction begins for each level of goal statement and for each goal. For example, if a general level goal is that the adult student will pass the GED test (cognitive goal) as a result of his program in the Adult Basic Education center, success could be measured by the adult's passing or not passing the GED test. If the intermediate level goal statement indicates that the adult will be able to type thirty words a minute with only two mistakes (psychomotor), the evaluation procedure and the criteria are evident; and measurement can take place. A specific level goal statement might be that the adult nurse's aide will be able to take the temperature of five different people and accurately record the temperatures on the patients' charts. Again, the goal and evaluation are clear and in consonance with one another. Stating the goal at any level requires that appropriate measures be specified so that adult student progress can continuously be checked. Goal statement and assessment procedures must go hand-in-hand in instruction and curriculum work.

Two different types of instruments or processes—norm-referenced or criterion-referenced—can be used to assess adult student performance. External *(norm-referenced)* tests have been developed outside the school and standardized for national or regional use. If the instructor is working with a group of adults on reading, he may specify that the students will be reading at the sixth-grade level when instruction is completed. Chances are the instructor will use some standardized test (external) to determine that the students have achieved that goal. The GED test is an example of a standardized test.

Besides using various externally developed instruments to assess adult student growth, many internal or *criterion-referenced* tests and procedures are used. These internal, generally teacher-made measures are designed to assess the achievement of adult students based on instructional goals developed by teacher and student. If, for example, the instructor states that adult students will be able to stitch the hem of a dress, or be able to solder an electrical circuit correctly, or be able to translate twenty-five words from Spanish to English, or be able to hand in accurate and neat accounting reports in a business class, the use of internally developed means of assessment to check behavior change would be most important. In any case, the instructor will determine what means of measurement is needed to assess goal statements.

Information about the growth of the adult student should be collected by the instructor and others during the learning experience, regardless of its length, and at the end of the experience. When an instructor collects information throughout a unit, semester, or year of study, he is collecting *formative* information. Formative data are important to see if the adult student is progressing well and to see if some changes in the program experiences are required to reach longer range goals. Gathering *summative* information at the end of the experience documents the total change in the adult student's behavior. Assessing where an adult is at the end of a longer instructional period will help the instructor, administrators, and others determine new directions for the adult student.

EVALUATION (Were the goals accomplished at three levels?)

Internal evidence	Formative information
External evidence	Summative information

Figure 3.3—**Evaluation**

The curriculum model now looks like this:

GOALS (What is worth learning in the adult view?)

General level—General, abstract
statements to cover longer
periods of time (i.e., programs,
years of study)

Intermediate level—More precise
statements to cover more manageable packages of instruction
(i.e., unit, semester, module,
year)

Specific level—Very precise
statements to cover daily
and short-term experiences
(i.e., daily lesson, short
topics)

Statements
specified
in
cognitive,
affective,
and
psychomotor
domains

INSTRUCTION ACTIVITIES (How will the goals be accomplished?)

Define terminal goals
Assess entering behavior
Define and organize content
Select materials
Invent and/or select strategies
Create classroom climate
Assess learning

EVALUATION (Were the goals accomplished at three levels?)

Internal evidence   Formative information
External evidence   Summative information

Figure 3.4—**Curriculum Design**

RATIONALE

The preceding three-part model would suffice as the design of a curriculum, regardless of the adult students involved, if the school operated in a social, cultural, and psychological vacuum. However, this is not the case. Curriculum developers interpret their total environment and begin to make judgments about what a curriculum should accomplish for their students and society. The rationale is the basis (the reason) for curriculum design and answers the question: "What do we believe about people, society, education, and our environment and their meaning for an educational program?" Answering questions in the following areas will aid the adult educator in developing a suitable curriculum for adult students:

1. *Nature of society*—What is it like and what meaning does it have for the adult and his program of experiences?
2. *Purposes of education*—Why do adults want education?
3. *Nature of the learner*—What is the adult learner like? What are his interests, needs, values, goals?
4. *Learning process*—How does learning take place in the adult and for what purpose?
5. *Knowledge and the curriculum*—What is the purpose of knowledge and how shall it be organized?
6. *Role of the professional adult educator*—What is the role of the adult educator in the classroom, in curriculum work, in the profession, and in society?

OUTSIDE POLITICAL FORCES

Outside forces come into play in developing the local curriculum. For the adult educator to build and maintain a productive and desirable curriculum for adult students, he must be aware of the outside political forces that affect his work. These forces are "outside" in the sense that they are not fostered within the local adult program, and they are "political" in the sense that they actually establish policy for the local program. Kirst and Walker (1971), in an excellent analysis of policy decision making, suggest that three main forces affect the curriculum. They are: (1) governmental agencies—local, state, federal; (2) private organizations—foundations, accrediting agencies, testing agencies, textbook companies; and (3) interest groups—NAACP, John Birch Society, National Association of Manufacturers. These agencies and organizations affect state and local curriculum policy making in the following ways:

1. *Groups that establish minimum curriculum standards*
   Accrediting agencies
   Testing agencies
   State departments of education
   Professional associations

2. *Groups that generate alternatives*
   Textbook companies
   Foundations
   Federal government
   Professional associations
   College and university professors
   Practicing teachers and administrators

3. *Groups that demand change (or no change) in the curriculum*
   Council for Basic Education
   National Association of Manufacturers
   AFL-CIO

It should be obvious to the adult instructor that the above-mentioned forces influence the content of the local adult curriculum. If the adult instructor wants his students to pass the GED test, the curriculum ought to address itself to those content areas found in the test. If accreditation is important to the local school, adherence to the standards specified by the accrediting agency is necessary. If one textbook or series of textbooks is adopted, it has a definite effect on the local curriculum. If an outside group demands that certain experiences be found in the curriculum and some of the adult students desire to work with that group, an instructor will need to consider some of their priorities. Finally, if a state or federal education agency provides funding based on certain requirements, the program will be designed to include the necessary components.

In the following curriculum model, the political forces component is placed between the rationale and the goals statement. Although a critical analysis by curriculum specialists can produce the initial rationale for the curriculum, outside forces must be considered before goals are stated and the curriculum developed.

The following general curriculum model contains all the elements discussed in this chapter.

RATIONALE   (What do we believe and feel about people, society, school and other environmental phenomena and their meaning for a school program?)
    Nature of society
    Purposes of education
    Nature of the learner
    Learning process
    Knowledge and curriculum
    Role of the professional educator

                           Governmental
      OUTSIDE POLITICAL FORCES   Private Organizations
                           Interest Group

GOALS   (What is worth learning in the adult view?)
      General level—General, abstract
        statements to cover longer
        periods of time (i.e., programs,
        years of study)

                              Statements
      Intermediate level—More precise   specified
        statements to cover more man-   in
        ageable packages of instruction   cognitive,
        (i.e., unit, semester, module,   affective,
        year)   and
                              psychomotor
      Specific level—Very precise   domains
        statements to cover daily
        and short-term experiences
        (i.e., daily lesson, short
        topics)

INSTRUCTION ACTIVITIES   (How will the goals be accomplished?)
        Define terminal goals
        Assess entering behavior
        Define and organize content
        Select materials
        Invent and/or select strategies
        Create classroom climate
        Assess learning

EVALUATION   (Were the goals accomplished at three levels?)
      Internal evidence   Formative information
      External evidence   Summative information

Figure 3.5—**General Curriculum Model**

SELECTED BIBLIOGRAPHY

Aker, B. L., & Poucell, T. *Developing and managing Adult Basic Education programs.*Tallahassee, Florida: Florida State University, March 1970. (ERIC Document Reproduction Service No. ED 054 441)

Axford, R. W. *Adult education: The open door.* Scranton, Pennsylvania: International Textbook Co., 1969.

Bergevin, P. E. *A philosophy for adult education.* New York: Seabury Press, 1967.

Boone, E. J., & Quinn, E. H. *Curriculum development in Adult Basic Education.* Chicago: Follett Education Corporation, 1967.

Hass, G., Bondi, J., & Wiles, J. *Curriculum planning: A new approach.* Boston: Allyn & Bacon, 1974.

Kirst, M. W., & Walker, D. F. An analysis of curriculum policy making. *Review of Educational Research,* 1971, *45* (5), 479-509.

Kneller, G. F. *Foundations of education.* New York: John Wiley & Sons, 1963.

Knowles, M. S. *The modern practice of adult education.* New York: Association Press, 1970.

Krathwohol, D. R. Stating objectives appropriately for program, for curriculum and for instructional materials development. *Journal of Teacher Education,* 1965, *16* (1), 83-92.

Kreitlow, B. W. *Educating the adult educator: Part I, Concepts for the curriculum.* Madison, Wisconsin: University of Wisconsin-Madison, March 1965.

Mezirow, J., Darkenwald, G. G., & Knox, A. B. *Last gamble on education.* Washington, D.C.: Adult Education Association of the U.S.A., 1975.

Miller, H. L. *Teaching and learning in adult education.* New York: Macmillan Co., 1969.

Nadler, L. *Developing human resources.* Houston, Texas: Gulf Publishing Co., 1970.

Rauch, D. B. (Ed.). *Priorities in adult education.* New York: Macmillan Co., 1972.

Saylor, J. G., & Alexander, W. *Planning curriculum for schools.* New York: Holt, Rinehart & Winston, 1974.

Sherk, J. K., Jr. *Curriculum design and organization—A new look.* Kansas City, Missouri: University of Missouri-Kansas City, February 1972.

Smith, R. M., Aker, G. F., & Kidd, J. R. (Eds.). *Handbook of adult education.* New York: Macmillan Co., 1970.

Taba, H. *Curriculum development theory and practice.* New York: Harcourt, Brace & World, 1962.

Tyler, R. W. *Principles of curriculum and instruction.* Chicago: University of Chicago Press, 1950.

Verduin, J. R., Jr. *Cooperative curriculum improvement.* Englewood Cliffs, New Jersey: Prentice-Hall, 1967.

4
Bases for General Goals in Adult Education

PHILOSOPHICAL BASE

The American educational system plays a vital role in bringing change and improvement to society, as well as providing a means for cultural preservation and transmission. Moreover, one of the reasons for America's vast and open educational system stems from an implicit understanding of the importance of an educated populace to the political structure of democracy. The educational system is based on the following beliefs:

1. *Belief in the dignity and worth of each individual*—Each person has the right to formulate his or her own ideas, the right to self-direction, and the right to live in society as an independent human being.

2. *Belief in the equality of human beings*—Although individuals do not possess equal capabilities or achievements, they are guaranteed the same rights and privileges that society has to offer. Among other things, this means that individuals can participate on an equal basis in making decisions affecting their own individual welfare.

3. *Belief in each person's ability to use reason*—The ideal of self-government is based upon the notion that if individuals use reason in determining solutions to problems, these solutions will, in the long run, be best not only for themselves but for society as well. Adults are capable of establishing their own goals in a rational manner.

4. *Belief in human perfectability*—The continuing efforts of individuals to improve themselves and their society have been one of the major forces in bettering their moral and material way of life.

5. *Belief in each human being's ability for self-governance*—The belief in the ability of individuals to govern themselves is a cornerstone of democracy. This assumes, of course, that individuals will approach participation in the democratic process on a rational basis and that they will make the necessary effort to become well informed about the issues confronting their society and welfare.

HISTORICAL BASE

Another influence in providing direction for adult education is its historical development which began more than two centuries ago. Without a doubt, the need for adult education took place the day settlers landed in Jamestown in 1607. In order to survive, the settlers had to learn to adapt to a new environment by such means as observation, trial and error, peer instruction, exchange of experiences, and tutoring. Their need for learning as effectively and as directly as possible was based on the pragmatic desire to survive.

Adult education during the early colonial experience was essentially informal, unorganized, and primarily devoted to learning life skills. The first settlers quickly formed such institutions as church study and worship groups, procedures for governmental decision making, and means for education. As divisions of labor emerged in established communities in the colonies, the system of apprenticeship offered the major form of vocational training. It was this system of mastering a commercial skill that formed the basis for job training, professional guilds, and other trade associations.

In 1728 Benjamin Franklin formed an organization called the Junto, which provided a distinct institutionalized effort among adults to share their knowledge with each other. Focusing on such topics as politics, morals, and natural philosophy, the Junto was based on the premise that each member would leave the parent organization and form a similar adult learning society, thus providing a network of adult communication and instruction. The Junto finally merged with the American Philosophical Society in 1769. The latter organization was to attract some of the best minds in the United States for the next half-century.

As a new nation was declared, fought for, and established, the task was to transform an entire people from subjects to citizens— from a people governed by an aristocracy in another land to a people able to govern themselves and able to determine their own fate among other nations of the world. No undertaking by any society ever staked more on the ability of adults to learn than did the founding of the Republic. The instruments by which this gigantic adult educational undertaking was accomplished were informal, voluntary, and decentralized. These included committees of correspondence, pamphlets, editorials, books, speeches, poems, plays, songs, and town meetings which explored the issues and ideas of democracy.

With nationhood achieved, the development of the library provided a vehicle for learning that was accessible to a wide audience. The earliest libraries, such as the Philadelphia Library Company, were operated upon the basis of a joint stock arrangement similar to a book club. The use of the library was based upon the payment of a subscription fee, the purchase of a share, or the purchase of an annual or lifetime membership. In several instances, it was a regular practice also to charge a fee for each book withdrawn. Another practice that was relatively common was to auction the most popular books to the highest bidder. The library concept grew rapidly. Thirty libraries, established between 1775 and 1800, contained approximately 242,171 volumes. An additional 551 libraries, containing a total of 2,807,218 volumes, were built between 1825 and 1850. The acceptance of a free public library did not develop until the last half of the nineteenth century. Massachusetts was one of the first to give legislative authority to the idea; in 1848 the city of Boston was empowered to raise $5,000 annually for the maintenance of a public library. Similar laws were enacted in other states within the next twenty-five years. The free public library was further established as a result of the philanthropic zeal of Andrew Carnegie who donated library buildings to cities throughout the country.

Like the library, the lyceum was available to a wide audience. Josiah Holbrook, a geologist from Derby, Connecticut, established the first lyceum in Massachusetts in 1826. In just thirteen years 3,000 lyceums were established throughout the nation. The lyceum sponsored weekly meetings and lectures; scientific demonstrations were often presented and discussed. While the lyceum was eventually to disappear, for a brief period it provided an educational service that was well received.

The Chautauqua Society, begun in 1874, served both an educational and recreational function. It was eventually to affect millions with a summer program in religion, discussion of public issues, book clubs, and presentations in music, art, theater, sports, and hobbies. An agency for securing lecturers was established. The Chautauqua Society grew out of Sunday School Teacher's Normal Assembly and was founded by Reverend John Heyl Vincent from New Jersey and Lewis Miller, an Akron businessman and inventor.

A further historical development was the correspondence school which was similar to the Chautauqua Society's use of reading lists. Correspondence schools began to flourish near the turn of the twentieth century to bring resources to adults who lived miles from any center of learning. The concept was even implemented on some university campuses. The University of Chicago established a program of correspondence and extension in 1892. Private businesses also established correspondence schools in a wide variety of subjects.

By 1920, many recognized that a large segment of the adult population had genuine educational needs. In 1924 the Carnegie Corporation held a conference on the topic, and under the leadership of Frederich P. Keppel, it decided to place priority on adult education. Two years later, the American Association for Adult Education was formed, strongly supported by the Carnegie Corporation. This association provided the adult education movement with an administrative structure, as well as a forum for discussion and a channel for dissemination of information.

While the creation of the American Association for Adult Education provided an administrative base to the movement, Professor E. L. Thorndike gave it intellectual credibility in 1928. Prior to that time, educators believed that the instruction of adults was a hopeless task. Speaking at the American Association for Adult Education, Thorndike reviewed several studies that he had conducted. His work demonstrated that while adults did not learn quite as rapidly as adolescents, they were educable. Thorndike suggested that the adult learner, for practical purposes, could master any subject that his adolescent counterpart could. Thorndike's work was published in a book entitled *Adult Learning* (1928). By his efforts, he altered the public's previous views toward adult education and provided an empirical base for its defense.

By the middle of the twentieth century self-enrichment adult education programs, adult vocational training, and adult programs for naturalization of immigrants were taking place through a variety of institutions and institutional arrangements. Active were organizations like the Citizenship Council of Metropolitan Chicago, which was founded by Helen G. Lynch for the purpose of assisting new Americans in becoming responsible citizens. Further, labor unions, professional organizations, and corporations had established ongoing adult training programs and schools.

LEGISLATIVE BASE

Much of the story of education and especially adult education can be understood by reviewing federal involvement in adult education. Some of the more significant legislation and executive action related to adult education are outlined below:

Year	Statute/Executive Order (if appropriate)	Provision
1777		Established military instruction of the Continental Army
1785	Land Ordinance	Reserved a section of land in territories for the support of schools
1787	Northwest Ordinance	Authorized land grants for the establishment of educational institutions
1800	Congressional Library	Began the book collection for the Library of Congress
1802	Military Academy	Established educational institution at West Point
1803	Ohio Enabling Act	Granted one square mile to each township in Ohio for the sole use of schools
1862	The Morrill Land Grant Act	Granted public land in each state for the support of a college for the enhancement of agriculture and mechanic arts and to provide military training
1867	Department of Education Act	Created the National Department of Education (later known as the Office of Education)

Year	Statute/Executive Order (if appropriate)	Provision
1897	Executive Order 9830	Established the Federal School for Engravers
1914	Smith-Lever Act	Provided federal assistance for extension training in home economics, agricultural production, and rural development
1914		Development of testing techniques and instructional programs for World War I recruits
1917	Smith-Hughes Act	Promoted vocational training and vocational trainer preparation
1918	Smith-Sears Act	Provided educational options for World War I veterans
1918	Immigration and Nationality Act	Established the Federal Immigration and Naturalization education services
1920	Smith-Bankhead Act	Formalized state and federal cooperation in the area of vocational rehabilitation
1929	George-Reed Act	Provided money over a five-year period for home economics and agricultural education
1933	Works Projects Administration	Provided funding for literacy education, general adult education, and vocational education
1936	George Deen Act	Expanded the Smith-Hughes Act
1941		Establishment of the United States Armed Forces Institute (USAFI)

Year	Statute/Executive Order (if appropriate)	Provision
1944	Servicemen's Readjustment Act (The G.I. Bill of Rights)	Granted assistance for the education of military veterans; permanent program provided in 1956
1944	Surplus Property Act	Initiated a policy of using government surplus for education, health, and civil defense
1946	George-Barden Act	Expanded federal-state vocational education with programs for practical nursing and fishery education
1955	Executive Order 9830	Provided for training of federal employees
1956	Library Services Act	Provided federal funds for library services to rural areas
1958	National Defense Education Act	Authorized funds to strengthen critical areas in education; provided for research and experimentation in teaching and improvement in statistical and information services
1961	Area Redevelopment Act	Provided assistance to individuals from economically depressed areas to increase their employability
1962	Manpower Development and Training Act	Established a program of occupational training and retraining of the American labor force utilizing the resources of industry, labor, educational institutions, and various agencies

Year	*Statute/Executive Order (if appropriate)*	*Provision*
1962	Educational TV Act All Channel TV Act	Provided funds for the construction of educational television stations
1963	Manpower Development and Training Amendment	Provided basic education programs for jobless illiterates seeking employment
1963	Higher Education Facilities Act	Provided a five-year program of federal grants and loans to colleges and universities for the expansion and new development of physical facilities
1964	Library Services and Construction Act	Extended federal financial assistance to urban as well as rural areas for library services and facilities for economically disadvantaged and institutionalized adults
1964	Economic Opportunity Act	Among other measures, provided for literacy and basic education for adults and provided for Volunteers in Service to America to develop volunteer services in mental health, migrant, Indian, and antipoverty programs
1966	Demonstration Cities and Metropolitan Development Act	Granted funds for the development of model neighborhoods and for educational services
1966	Adult Education Act	Expanded basic educational programs for adults to enable them to overcome English language limitations and to

Year	Statute/Executive Order (if appropriate)	Provision
		improve their basic education in preparation for occupational training and more profitable employment
1967	Public Broadcasting Act	Created the Corporation for Public Broadcasting
1968	Vocational Education Amendments	Expanded federal vocational education programs with job preparation as a major goal
1969	Executive Order 11478	Required affirmative action to insure equal employment for federal employees, also provided training programs for employees to facilitate their advancement
1970	Arts and Humanities Extension	Extended the National Foundation for the Arts and Humanities for three years
1970	Comprehensive Drug Abuse Prevention and Control Act	Authorized funds to reach, treat, and rehabilitate drug dependent persons through community-oriented programs
1970	Environmental Quality Education Act	Provided funds for environmental education with a small grant provision for civic and volunteer organizations
1971	Emergency Employment Act	Authorized funds to state and local communities for public service programs during times of high unemployment

Year	Statute/Executive Order (if appropriate)	Provision
1973	The Comprehensive Employment and Training Act	Provided funds for job training and other services leading to employment and self-sufficiency
1973	Older Americans Comprehensive Services Amendment	Made available to older citizens comprehensive programs of health, education, and social services
1974	Elementary & Secondary Education Act Amendment, Title IV	Provided funding for community education programs and established the federal Community Education Advisory Council
1976	Higher Education Act Amendment, Title I	Established a new program of lifelong learning for adults who have left the traditionally sequenced education system

What does this brief review of legislation and federal involvement mean for adult education? One primary objective of adult education legislation is to prepare and retrain adults for socioeconomic self-sufficiency and meaningful employment. In addition, a review of the legislation reflects that adult education tends to be project oriented for a specified period of time and for a specific target population. Such defined programs place great emphasis on the undereducated and the underemployed. Adult education legislation typically involves categorical grant-in-aid funding. This means that the legislation contains specific guidelines as to how the allocated money is to be used and administered by state and local education agencies. These grants may be funded on a formula basis and require state or local matching funds or they may be funded based on project needs as documented in the grant application process.

From this brief review of the philosophical tenets, the historical movements, and the legislative bases of adult education, the adult educator can gain a sense of where adult education has been, where it currently is, and where it might be going in the future. Adult educators need to give careful thought to future requirements and directions in the field. This analysis will in turn lead to the development of new directions and goals for all participants involved in adult instruction.

SELECTED BIBLIOGRAPHY

Adams, D. A. *Review and synthesis of research concerning adult vocational and technical education.* Columbus, Ohio: ERIC Clearinghouse on Vocational and Technical Education, 1972. (ERIC Document Reproduction Service No. ED 064 469)

American Vocational Association, Post-Secondary Section. Making the case for adult education: In theory and practice. *American Vocational Journal,* 1970, *45* (2), 78-82.

Axford, R. W. *Adult education: The open door.* Scranton, Pennsylvania: International Textbook Co., 1969.

Bailey S. K. Educational purpose and the pursuit of happiness. *Phi Delta Kappan,* 1976, *58* (1), 42-47.

Benson, C. S. *The cheerful prospect: A statement on the future of American education.* Boston: Houghton Mifflin Co., 1965.

Bostwick, A. E. *The American public library.* New York: D. Appleton & Co., 1910.

Ciavareila, M. A. *Community education funding guide.* Shippensburg, Pennsylvania: Shippensburg State College, Commonwealth Center for Community Education, March 1977

Congressional Quarterly Service. *Federal role in education.* Washington, D.C.: Author, 1969.

Dulles, F. S. *America learns to play.* New York: D. Appleton-Century Co., 1940.

Federal programs for education and related activities. In U.S. National Center for Education Statistics, *Digest of education statistics — 1975.* Washington, D.C.: Government Printing Office, 1976.

Frohlicher, J. S., & Jennings, J. F. The Federal approach to education: What happens after the November elections? *Phi Delta Kappan,* 1976, *58* (2), 179-180.

Hiemstra, R. *Lifelong learning.* Lincoln: Professional Educators Publications, 1976.

Johnson, E. D. *A history of libraries in the Western world.* New York: Scarecrow Press, 1970.

Knowles, M. (Ed.). *Handbook of adult education.* Chicago: Adult Education Association of the U.S.A., 1960.

Lapati, A. D. *Education and the federal government: A historical record.* New York: Mason Charter, 1975.

McClusky, H. Y. Adult dimensions of lifelong learning: Reflections on the future of the educational enterprise. *Innovator,* 1976, *7* (9), 11-12.

Miller, H. G., & Greer, C. E. Developing adult education programs—Why? how? *Illinois School Board Journal,* 1973, *41* (1), 20-22.

Nystrom, D. C. *Occupation and career education legislation.* Indianapolis: Howard W. Sams & Co., 1973.

Rauch, D. B. (Ed.). *Priorities in adult education.* New York: Macmillan Co., 1972.

The Spectator; Journal of the National University Extension Association, 1976, *40* (24).

Thorndike, E. L., Bregman, E. O., Tilton, W. J., & Woodyard, E. *Adult learning.* New York: Macmillan Co., 1928.

Ulin, J. K. *The Adult Education Act 1964 - 1974: An historical perspective.* Washington, D.C.: U.S. National Advisory Council on Adult Education, 1976.

Venn, G. *Man, education and manpower.* Washington, D.C.: American Association of School Administrators, 1970.

5

Model for Adult Instruction

A dult instruction is the delivery system for a curriculum, program, project, or unit of study, involving careful planning as well as the actual instructional interaction with adult students. Because of its importance in the total curriculum and because of its relationship to adult students and their behavior, instruction requires very careful attention. A general model of adult instruction will be presented in this chapter with discussion for use. More in-depth discussion on various components of this model will occur in later chapters.

OVERVIEW OF THE MODEL

The instruction process for adults should begin with two important procedures: (1) assessing the entering behavior of the adult student, and (2) defining student and class goals to be achieved in the learning effort. These two operations should take place in conjunction with one another so that adult students can have goals (however defined) which are attainable according to their previous learning levels and experiences. If the goals held by adults are too difficult to attain, adults may experience considerable frustration causing dropouts from the program. If the goals do not present a challenge or require new learning, adult students may feel that they are wasting valuable time.

Once the goals have been carefully identified and stated, the teacher defines and outlines content to achieve the goals. Instructional procedures are selected, materials are identified, and learning tasks are developed and sequenced for effective learning. These three processes—assessing entering behavior, specifying objectives, and defining the learning unit and procedures—may be viewed as the planning phase of the instructional process. These generally occur before moving into the classroom or the instructional setting for the actual teaching of adults.

The second phase of the instructional model involves classroom operations—the direct interaction among students, teachers, and content. While presenting learning tasks to adult students, the teacher needs to establish a positive, supportive learning climate. Teachers of adults must be aware of their communication patterns—both verbal and nonverbal—to insure that a supportive, secure climate is established. Certain supportive words, a smile, a frown, ignoring a raised hand, a pat on the shoulder can do much to build or destroy a positive learning climate in an adult education learning situation.

As the adult student performs the learning tasks, the teacher keeps in close contact to review performance and get and give appropriate feedback as to success or lack of success in learning. Without such frequent feedback the adult teacher is unable to assess performance and move the adult student to new levels of learning or to modify the learning situation so that adults can acquire the stated objectives.

The general instructional model emphasizes an individualization of the instructional process. Each adult student comes to the learning experience with different levels of entering behavior and different goals or objectives to be attained. This, in turn, requires different learning units and interactions so that each adult can acquire new behaviors appropriate to his or her needs and capabilities. Individualizing instruction for adults is not an easy task, but it affords the best possible learning experiences for each adult.

The instructional model which follows includes all the components discussed in this chapter.

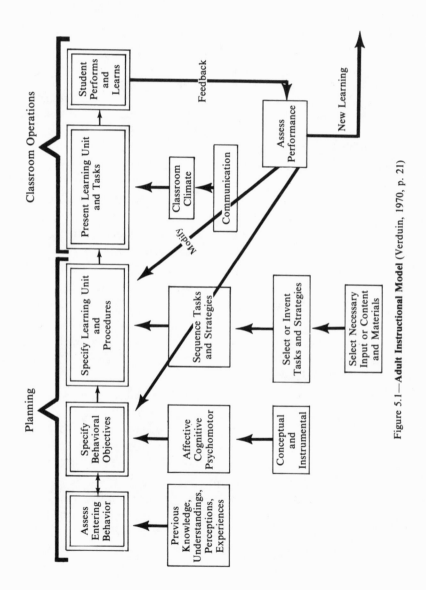

Figure 5.1—**Adult Instructional Model** (Verduin, 1970, p. 21)

ASSESSING ENTERING BEHAVIOR AND SPECIFYING OBJECTIVES

The entering behavior or performance of the adults is the level of knowledge and skill that adults bring to the new instruction. De Cecco (1968, p. 59) states that

entering behavior describes the behaviors the student must have acquired before he can acquire particular new terminal behaviors. More simply, entering behavior describes the present status of the student's knowledge and skill in reference to a future status the teacher wants him to attain. Entering behavior, therefore, is where the instruction must always begin.

Measuring the student's behavior or level of performance is necessary because the adult teacher's job is to move the adult student from entering performance to that of the desired terminal performance (the objective). Many times the entering performances for new instruction are the end products of previous instruction. Teachers can make the assessment of entering behaviors easier and more precise by listing the needed performances for the new instruction. Listing requisite behaviors is important and as De Cecco (1968, p. 59) suggests:

A list of entering behavior reveals two characteristics: The statements are explicit and refer to specific, observable performances and the list as a whole is generally more comprehensive than the corresponding list of terminal performances.

There are other personal qualities affecting an adult's learning abilities besides those of previous skill development and performance levels. The adult teacher, when assessing entering behavior, should look at an adult's motivation, personal goals, readiness, past experiences, socio-cultural values and beliefs, and current life situation. As suggested in an earlier chapter, a careful review of the adult's total perceptual and behavioral "package" is needed so that all learning experiences will have meaning for the adult and will influence and change his behavior. A well-developed student profile will serve as the basis for all subsequent educational activities of the individual adult. With this baseline information available the adult instructor can then assess learning levels and performances for individual areas of study.

With the assessment of entering levels of performance comes the specification of objectives for the learning unit. Instructional objectives, the kinds of behaviors that students should display at the end of a learning unit, obviously provide the direction for the formal instruction and are central to the instructional process. The use and treatment of objectives will occur in more depth in the following chapter. However, it is important to stress here that goal statements must be carefully defined at the beginning or a breakdown in the instructional process occurs before it actually starts. Mager (1962, p. 3) argues this point by stating:

> When clearly defined goals are lacking, it is impossible to evaluate a course or program efficiently, and there is no sound basis for selecting appropriate materials, content, or instructional methods. After all, the machinist does not select a tool until he knows what operation he intends to perform. Neither does a composer orchestrate a score until he knows what effects he wishes to achieve. Similarly, a builder does not select his materials or specify a schedule for construction until he has his blueprints (objectives) before him. Too often, however, one hears teachers arguing the relative merits of textbooks or other aids or the classroom versus the laboratory, without ever specifying just what goal the aid or method is to assist in achieving. I cannot emphasize too strongly the point that an instructor will function in a fog of his own making until he knows just what he wants his students to be able to do at the end of the instruction.

Instrumental and Conceptual Goals

Once the adult instructor sees the importance of clear, concise goal statements for the entire instructional process, he must then think about the relationship of objectives to the content area that will be taught. Every teaching activity has some content which influences adult students through their interaction with it. The teacher provides the various environmental conditions, both real and simulated, to which the adult student reacts. The environmental conditions will vary with the kind of behavior desired whether simple or very complex.

In the case of rather simple behaviors, which are largely reflex actions, *instrumental behavior* can be developed through various forms of operant conditioning. This major category of behaviors requires little in the way of logical, conceptual content, so a form of conditioning will effect the desired behavior. Examples of behavior in this category are: (1) adding several three-digit numbers within ten seconds, (2) responding to a picture of a horse by writing the word *horse,* (3) using proper grammatical expressions, (4) spelling the English language correctly, and (5) translating foreign words into English. Numerous items are learned in an adult classroom which do not require the adult to have direct exposure or contact with the environment to learn. It should be noted by the adult instructor that these behaviors in the instrumental category are important and should not be slighted. However, designing learning units for their acquisition is different from that of conceptual objectives.

Besides these rather simple instrumental behavioral objectives, the adult student needs to learn about many other behaviors which are more complex in nature, such as welding, nursing, the United States Constitution, getting a job, keeping a checkbook, real estate, and home tailoring. This more complex behavior involves specifying *conceptual goals* and, in turn, providing for the adult student's interaction with a certain environmental condition. The adult perceives the objects and events in the environment, forms concepts about them, uses the concepts for making decisions, and acts on these decisions. These conceptual goals are, therefore, important because an adult student's environment is composed of objects (structural concepts) and events (process objectives). Forming concepts about objects and events gives the adult the raw material with which to think about, judge, and act upon his world.

Woodruff (1964) defines a concept as

> a relatively complete and meaningful idea in the mind of a person. It is an understanding of something. It is his own subjective product of his way of making meaning of things he has seen or otherwise perceived

in his experiences. At its most concrete level it is likely to be a mental image of some actual object or event the person has seen. At its most abstract and complex level it is a synthesis of a number of conclusions he has drawn about his experiences with particular things.

He defines a *process concept* as "a concept of a process, event or behavior and the consequences it produces when it occurs" and a *structural concept* as "a concept of an object, relationship or structure of some kind" (Woodruff, 1964).

Examples of process concepts and their proper form are as follows:

When the surfaces of the parts of certain metals are heated and are allowed to flow together, the metallic parts will unite (welding concept).

If the United States Senate and House of Representatives pass a bill and the President signs it, it then becomes law (Constitutional concept).

When an adult teacher specifies the content to be taught in a classroom in terms of conceptual statements, the actual teaching task is made easier because the direction is much clearer (teaching concept).

Examples of structural concepts include:

A bill of sale is a formal instrument for the conveyance or transfer of title to various goods or properties (business concept).

The normal body temperature of a human being is approximately 98.6° F (nursing concept).

An instructional model brings into consideration some thought about entering behavior, goal statements, the learning unit and procedures, the presentation of the learning unit, adult performance of tasks, and assessment of outcomes (teaching concept).

The values derived from specifying and utilizing these kinds of conceptual goals are many. First, the two major types, process and structural, actually describe all events and objects in an adult learner's environment and thus cover the content or knowledge variable with a high degree of precision. In other words, what adults should learn about their world can be stated precisely in these forms. Secondly, when stated correctly, these conceptual statements make explicit the direction, the materials, and the content of the learning unit. If, for example, an adult instructor wants his beginning welding students to learn the following bit of knowledge—"When you heat the surfaces of the parts of certain metals and allow them to flow together, the metallic parts will unite" (a beginning process concept)—the instructor has before him the content that must be used, the materials that are necessary, and the exact direction that instruction will take. This simplifies the instructional process and adds power because the concept dictates the content that will be used.

Finally, upon specifying the conceptual goals, the adult teacher can further translate these into overt behaviors that the adults will display at the end of the learning unit. In the above example on welding, the adult instructor may have the adults simply describe this process on paper (a knowledge level objective in the cognitive domain) or actually perform the process with appropriate equipment and materials (an overt behavior in the psychomotor domain). In either case the adult instructor can see evidence that the adult has learned this content. Conceptual goals (content or knowledge) are compatible with behavioral goals (behaviors) because the adult teacher can list the behavioral goals that adults will possess after they have interacted with their environment. Power and precision are thus added to the instructional process because of this basic compatibility of educational goals.

Goals in the Cognitive, Affective, and Psychomotor Domains

Instructional objectives can be divided into three major areas: cognitive, affective, and psychomotor. Since the instructor's job is to assist the adult student to acquire new behaviors, it is helpful to think in terms of these three major domains of educational objectives. Published taxonomies (or category systems) occur in two domains: the cognitive (Bloom et al., 1956) and the affective (Krathwohl, Bloom, & Masia, 1964). Some attempts exist in the psychomotor domain, but these are without the precision of the first two (Simpson, 1966).

The *cognitive domain* is divided into a knowledge category and five categories which involve the skills and abilities needed to use this knowledge. A brief outline of the cognitive domain follows (Bloom et al., 1956):

1.00 *Knowledge*
    1.10 Knowledge of specifics
        1.11 Knowledge of terminology
        1.12 Knowledge of specific facts
    1.20 Knowledge of ways and means of dealing with specifics
        1.21 Knowledge of conventions
        1.22 Knowledge of trends and sequences
        1.23 Knowledge of classifications and categories
        1.24 Knowledge of criteria
        1.25 Knowledge of methodology
    1.30 Knowledge of the universals and abstractions in a field
        1.31 Knowledge of principles and generalizations
        1.32 Knowledge of theories and structures
2.00 *Comprehensions*
    2.10 Translations
    2.20 Interpretation
    2.30 Extrapolation
3.00 *Application*
4.00 *Analysis*
    4.10 Analysis of elements
    4.20 Analysis of relationships
    4.30 Analysis of organizational principles
5.00 *Synthesis*
    5.10 Production of unique communication
    5.20 Production of a plan, or proposed set of operations
    5.30 Derivation of a set of abstract relations

6.00   *Evaluation*
   6.10   Judgments in terms of internal evidence
   6.20   Judgments in terms of external criteria

This taxonomy is hierarchical in nature, because each category is built on the previous category. In other words, one must know about something (knowledge) before he can understand it (comprehension), he must understand it (comprehension) before he can apply it (application), and on up the continuum. Krathwohl (1965, p. 87) states:

> Perhaps the idea of a continuum is most easily gained from looking at the major headings of the cognitive domain, which include knowledge (recall of facts, principles, etc.), comprehension (ability to restate knowledge in new words), application (the ability to apply information to new situations), analysis (understanding well enough to break it apart into its parts and make the relations among ideas explicit), synthesis (the ability to produce wholes from parts, to produce a plan of operation, to derive a set of abstract relations), and evaluation (the ability to judge the value of material for given purposes).

The *affective domain* or system is actually based on an "internalization" idea. "Internalization in this case means the change or inner growth that occurs in an individual as he becomes aware of and adopts certain attitudes and principles which are inherent in forming selected judgments and behaving according to his values" (Verduin, 1967, p. 119).

A brief outline of the affective taxonomy (Krathwohl et al., 1964, p. 35) is as follows:

1.00   *Receiving (attending)*
   1.10   Awareness
   1.20   Willingness to receive
   1.30   Controlled or selected attention
2.00   *Responding*
   2.10   Acquiescence in responding
   2.20   Willingness to respond
   2.30   Satisfaction in response

3.00 *Valuing*
    3.10 Acceptance of a value
    3.20 Preference for a value
    3.30 Commitment
4.00 *Organization*
    4.10 Conceptualization
    4.20 Organization of a value system
5.00 *Characterization by a value or value complex*
    5.10 Generalized set
    5.20 Characterization

According to this system the adult student will receive stimuli in a classroom learning situation which begin to change his affective behavior. As the adult begins to respond to the stimuli, he is becoming emotionally involved and will attach some personal significance to what is taking place. If the internalization process continues, the adult will begin to hold certain values about the object or event under consideration. At this point in an adult's affective behavior, several relevant values may enter into the internalization process; and the adult will begin to conceptualize and organize the many values involved. Finally, the internalization process reaches a point at which the adult will continually respond to value-oriented situations with a new and consistent view of his environment and world. The total behavior will then be characterized by a consistent set of actions which may be described as a philosophy of life.

It is no easy task for the adult student to integrate a set of values into a philosophy of life. This may take several years or may not occur at all. However difficult it may be, adult teachers must be aware of this internalization process because many affective behaviors are required for successful living in society.

Students also form attitudes about the instructional situation and about the cognitive and psychomotor skills they are learning. For example, as the reader peruses this book, he or she is going through a cognitive experience but is also forming some judgments as to its value or lack of value. Teachers should present learning experiences in ways that will appeal to, rather than discourage, students.

Although little has been done in categorizing the *psychomotor domain,* the following model of one category system and its various processes should provide some assistance to the adult instructor:

OBSERVATION
(Individual watches process
and pays attention to steps
and to finished product.)

↓

IMITATION
(Individual follows directions
and carries out steps with
conscious awareness. May
perform hesitantly.)

↓

PRACTICE
(Individual repeats steps until
some or all aspects become
habitual, and performs the
process smoothly.)

↓

ADAPTATION
(Individual modifies and
adapts to suit himself
or the situation.)

Figure 5.2—**Psychomotor Categories**

The first process in the development of a psychomotor skill is observation. The adult student watches the psychomotor skill, paying close attention to the steps and the finished product. Next comes imitation whereby the student follows directions and carries out with awareness the steps in the skill area. Imitation assumes observation or previous reading of directions. The third psychomotor category is practice. The student repeats the steps until some or all aspects of the process become habitual requiring little conscious effort. Practice should occur until the adult student can perform the skill smoothly. This category requires prior imitation and observation or reading. The final category is adaptation. At this stage the skill has been acquired and can be used or transferred to new and unique situations. Adult learners make individual modifications and adaptations in the process skill to suit themselves and the situation.

The category system, however, does not fix standards of quality or performance. The adult instructor after a careful review of the skill area can specify what quality standards are required for success. These standards can be worked into the practice and adaptation categories as the adult student gains the appropriate psychomotor behaviors.

DESIGNING LEARNING UNITS AND PROCEDURES

Once the goals for the learning unit have been carefully considered and clearly stated, the adult teacher has an exact direction for the development of the learning unit. If the final behavioral goals are very explicit, the nature of the content and materials is right before the adult teacher. (If the teacher of English as a Second Language wishes to have as a performance the correct pronunciation of twenty words in English, the content and materials are present.)

In all cases, then, the content and materials are dictated by the goals; content and materials do not dictate the direction of the learning unit. The strategies and learning tasks are also dictated by the goal statements. If a teacher wants students to apply basic information on water pollution to specific community problems, he must provide tasks that will elicit application. If the adult teacher wants students to add numbers in two columns, the strategy and tasks are quite apparent.

In cases where more than one goal has been stated, it will become necessary to organize and sequence the tasks to be presented. Generally, basic concept formation precedes application of the new concepts. If several concepts are involved in developing a principle, organization must occur in the treatment of the concepts. Presenting the concepts in some logical order will aid adults in their learning efforts.

In developing a learning unit it is necessary to assess the amount and kind of direct sensory intake that has occurred prior to the new learning. For example, it would be very difficult for adults to use a clinical thermometer and understand the concept of body temperature if they have not had any direct contact with the instrument and its nature. Adults would have to see the instrument, its gradations, and operation before any further learning activity could occur. Normally, no amount of verbage will accomplish this direct sensory input. It would also be difficult to apply various concepts on lumber in a building class until adults have actually seen the kinds and sizes of lumber available for use. If, however, adults do have this basic input, then it is not necessary to provide this sensory experience. A careful assessment is required to ascertain what adults have actually perceived in their experiences with their environment.

A final consideration in designing a learning unit based on specified goals is that of time required for learning. All adults in a classroom possess unique individual differences; some will learn more quickly than others. The adult instructor needs to allow for these differences in terms of time to complete the various tasks.

PRESENTING LEARNING UNITS AND
CREATING A LEARNING CLIMATE

Considerable attention is devoted to methods and techniques of instruction in future chapters, so this section will focus on building and maintaining a positive, secure classroom climate in which adults can learn and acquire new behaviors. In reviewing existing evidence on school classrooms and teacher behavior, Gage indicates that a highly desirable characteristic of teachers is "teacher warmth." Gage (1968, p. 402) has found that effective teachers "tend to behave approvingly, acceptantly, and supportively; they tend to speak well of their own pupils, pupils in general, and people in general. They tend to like and trust rather than fear other people of all kinds." Since many adult learners see the classroom as a threatening place—not associated with success—these teacher qualities are especially important for effective learning and retention of students.

The climate established in a classroom is based on verbal and nonverbal communication. What the teacher says can set a tone or pattern of interaction which can encourage or discourage student participation. Dominant teacher talk, lack of praise, ignoring students' ideas, criticizing, and not asking questions will inhibit student involvement in a classroom. On the other hand, verbal statements that bring students into the discussion and involve them in interaction can encourage the adult learner and make him feel an important part of the learning situation.

Nonverbal behavior by the adult teacher can also encourage or inhibit involvement by the student. Teacher-initiated moves, such as responding to a raised hand or a puzzled look, will build climate. Such positive expressions as enthusiasm and liking the students will do more than expressions that convey aloofness, coldness, low regard, and indifference. Listening to students with patience and interest shows more warmth than inattentive or disinterested expressions. Helping a student who is having difficulty is better than ignoring the student when a response would ordinarily be expected. Finally, expressions that support students, manifest approval, exhibit encouragement, and connote enjoyment or praise will aid more in climate building than expressions of dissatisfaction, discouragement, disparagement, or punishment.

Verbal expressions and nonverbal movements send messages to adult students. It is important that these messages convey support, acceptance, responsiveness, and positive regard. The adult student learns best when he feels secure (Maurer, 1969).

ADULT PERFORMANCE, FEEDBACK, AND ASSESSMENT

As the adult student performs the various tasks in a learning unit, adult instructors and students must gather feedback to assess the level of performance and achievement taking place through many methods. Again, the goals or objectives of the learning experience should be so stated that the adult teacher can begin to look for the overt behavior or products of behavior that have resulted from the experience. From a simple observation to an extended review of some written work or other product by the adult student, the teacher can gather the necessary information to assess the level of performance of the adult. Some goals may be assessed immediately; others may take longer. In any case, the teacher must be aware of the performance level so he can modify some goals, experiences, or presentations if difficulty arises or have the student move on to new learning experiences. If changes are necessary and of an immediate nature, the teacher can foster these changes quickly or add new input; and the student can proceed to achieve. The final dimension of the model lends more precision to the instructional act and provides some accountability as to teacher performance and adult learner performance. More discussion on assessment and evaluation occurs in future chapters.

SELECTED BIBLIOGRAPHY

Bloom, B. S., et al. *Taxonomy of educational objectives, the classification of educational goals, handbook I: Cognitive domain.* New York: David McKay, 1956.

Davis, L. N., & McCallon, E. *Planning, conducting and evaluating workshops.* Austin, Texas: Learning Concepts, 1974.

DeCecco, J. P. *The psychology of learning and instruction: Educational psychology.* Englewood Cliffs, New Jersey: Prentice-Hall, 1968.

Dickinson, G. *Teaching adults: A handbook for instructors.* Toronto: New Press, 1973.

Dubin, S. S., & Okun, M. Implications of learning theories for adult instruction. *Adult Education,* 1973, *24* (1), 3-9.

Ennis, R. H. *Logic in teaching.* Englewood Cliffs, New Jersey: Prentice-Hall, 1969.

Gage, N. L. (Ed.). *Handbook of research on teaching.* Chicago: Rand McNally, 1963.

Gage, N. L. Can science contribute to the art of teaching? *Phi Delta Kappan,* 1968, *49* (7), 399-403.

Harrow, A. J. *A taxonomy of the psychomotor domain; a guide for developing behavioral objectives.* New York: David McKay, 1972.

Joyce, B., & Weil, M. *Models of teaching.* Englewood Cliffs, New Jersey: Prentice-Hall, 1972.

Kibler, R. J., Barker, L. L., & Miles, D. T. *Behavioral objectives and instruction.* Boston: Allyn & Bacon, 1970.

Klevins, C. (Ed.). *Materials and methods in adult education.* New York: Klevens Publications, 1972.

Krathwohl, D. R. Stating objectives appropriately for programs, for curriculum, and for instructional materials development. *Journal of Teacher Education,* 1965, *16* (1), 83-92.

Krathwohl, D. R., Bloom, B. S., & Masia, B. *Taxonomy of educational objectives, the classification of educational goals, handbook II: Affective domain.* New York: David McKay, 1964.

Mager, R. F. *Preparing instructional objectives.* Palo Alto, California: Fearon Publishers, 1962.

Mager, R. F., & Beach, K. M. *Developing vocational instruction.* Belmont, California: Fearon Publishers, 1967.

Maurer, N. S. (Ed.). *Tips for teaching textiles and clothing.* Albany: New York State Education Department, Bureau of Continuing Education Curriculum Services, 1969. (ERIC Document Reproduction Service No. ED 044 589)

Miller, H. L. *Teaching and learning in adult education.* New York: Macmillan Co., 1969.

Popham, W. J., & Baker, E. L. *Systematic instruction.* Englewood Cliffs, New Jersey: Prentice-Hall, 1970.

Simpson, E. J. *The classification of educational objectives, psychomotor domain.* Unpublished manuscript, University of Illinois, 1966.

Verduin, J. R., Jr. *Conceptual models in teacher education.* Washington, D.C.: American Association of Colleges for Teacher Education, 1967.

Verduin, J. R., Jr., & Heinz, C. R. *Pre-student teaching laboratory experiences.* Dubuque, Iowa: Kendall-Hunt Publishing Co., 1970.

Verner, C., & Booth, A. *Adult education.* New York: Center for Applied Research in Education, 1964.

Woodruff, A. D. *Putting subject matter into conceptual form.* Paper prepared for TEAM Project meeting, American Association of Colleges for Teacher Education, Washington, D.C., February 6, 1964.

6

Specifying Objectives for Adult Instruction

Objectives are the direction-giving element in the entire instructional process. Everything else should be contingent on the objectives that are specified. This chapter will discuss the uses, levels, and selection of objectives for adult instruction and will conclude with a section on behavioral objectives.

USE OF OBJECTIVES

Objectives are the key to a successful adult instructional program. Objectives are goals, aims, or intentions for achieving desired educational outcomes through a curriculum, a program, or a course. Since objectives are descriptive statements of prospective outcomes, they give direction to the resources that are available so that adults can learn as effectively, efficiently, and accurately as possible.

Objectives typically serve the following purposes:

1. To provide direction for an educational institution in terms of programs and use of resources

2. To direct or guide the adult teacher in preparing content, structuring learning experiences, and selecting materials for classroom teaching
3. To provide direction for the adult student in the learning process
4. To guide program and curriculum development in terms of content, materials, learning experiences, and organization for instruction
5. To provide a criterion base for diagnosis
6. To provide a means by which evaluation of instruction and learning can be measured
7. To provide statements that are either explicitly or implicitly related to the behavior change that is desired
8. To provide guidance in the process of assigning priorities for resources, personnel, instructional time, and content
9. To inform the public, funding agency, or school board of the institution's purposes and programs
10. To provide a guide concerning what and how to teach

The overall purpose for having objectives is to provide instructional direction and a means for measuring the effects of the instruction on adult students. When objectives are not developed, instructional planning and teaching are left to change; and the possibility of program failure is increased.

LEVELS OF OBJECTIVES

Objectives may be written at five different educational levels, as seen in Figure 6.1. The first level pertains to the broad educational priorities of society. Education should assist adults in their continuing efforts to realize their potential. In some instances, the objective is stated in a specific piece of legislation, such as the 1973 Comprehensive Employment and Training Act, which provides job training and employment opportunities for adults. In other cases, it is implied through the existence of self-enrichment and rehabilitation programs.

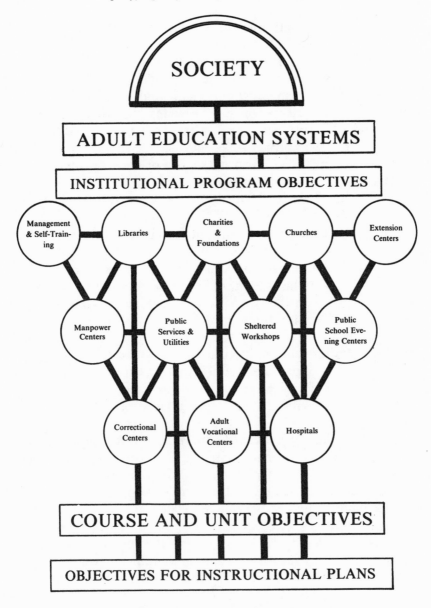

Figure 6.1—**Levels of Objectives**

A second level of educational objectives pertains to adult educational systems. Many institutions and single programs for adults function within a system, such as the state and federal correctional systems. Programs for the elderly, adult programs operating within public schools, and adult library programs function within systems which are directed by their own system goals and objectives. In some instances, these objectives are mandated by law; at other times they may be self-imposed. Two different systems may have very similar or identical objectives; for example, an adult bilingual program may be funded to prepare adults for immediate employment and may have the same objective as a manpower program.

Objectives stated for an institution, whether a center, school, agency, community college, or university, constitute a third level of objectives. Adult instruction may be a major part or even the total mission of an institution, or it may be only one aspect of an institution's responsibility. A correctional facility has a dual mission; rehabilitation through education is only one aspect. On the other hand, an adult vocational center or a division of continuing education is primarily an instructional institution. Because institutions typically house several distinct programs and services, objectives at this level tend to remain broad in scope and long-term in nature. They correspond to the general level of objectives in the curriculum model (Figure 3.6).

Course or unit objectives (the fourth level) are generally more specific and include the components needed to achieve the overall objectives. A program represents (1) several courses which may include sequences, such as Welding I and Welding II; or (2) courses which are nonsequenced but content related, such as ceramics and poetry. Programs may be sponsored by an institution but offered at times convenient to adults in a variety of community locations. Homes, churches, businesses, community centers, hospitals, and public and private schools are typical sites. This level corresponds to the intermediate level in the curriculum model (Figure 3.6).

Writing objectives for instructional plans (the fifth level) is one of the most important instructional responsibilities of an adult educator. Instructional objectives can be written for an entire class or for an individual adult. They specify the type of instruction and the instructional resources needed. In addition, they provide criteria for determining adult student and teacher success. This level is similar to the specific level of objectives in the curriculum model (Figure 3.6).

SELECTION OF OBJECTIVES

The teacher develops instructional objectives within the context of the broader goals of the program, the institution, and society. In addition, the instructor needs to determine specific course content based on adult goals and job performance requirements. Several approaches can be used to gather and select course content.

One approach is to observe and interview people performing tasks being considered for inclusion in the course. The following questions are pertinent:

What is the person doing?
How does the person perform various tasks?
Under what conditions and with what equipment does the person accomplish a task?
How does the person perceive a task he/she is performing?
What errors have been made?
What needs to be improved?
What would the person do differently?

After analyzing and describing the tasks, the observer compiles a list of skills needed to perform the activity correctly. A beautician may demonstrate such tasks as cutting, shampooing, shaping, and combing. A chef baking a soufflé may demonstrate the use of special cooking utensils, the use of an oven, and techniques to determine whether the soufflé is ready. An approach based upon what is occurring assumes that the persons being observed are conscious of what they are doing and why. Furthermore, length and number of observations, variety of tasks being performed, expertise of the observed and observer, and accuracy in describing situations are all important to the documentation process.

A second approach frequently used to determine appropriate tasks is to survey those tasks which professionals and professional organizations recommend for inclusion in a learning experience. In teaching a beginning typing course, the question should be: "What makes a good typist?" Professional organizations have typically formulated job standards, codes, and classification schemes for approved members. Unions provide for various levels of recognition and licensing in many vocational areas.

In a third frequently used approach adult teachers use their own experiences to determine what should be taught. The quality, variety, and length of experiences of adult teachers are factors in determining what is perceived as important. Examples of task expectations of vocational directors are described in the following fashion.

1. Vocational directors collect and analyze labor market and employment data for program development.
2. Vocational directors analyze program success by comparing job opportunities and job placement.
3. Vocational directors use local advisory committees made up of business people from the community.
4. Vocational directors prepare news releases concerning their program.
5. Vocational directors write and use newsletters.
6. Vocational directors write guidelines for evaluating instructional staff.
7. Vocational directors conduct action research regarding the program.
8. Vocational directors write proposals for state/federal reimbursement for programs and projects.
9. Vocational directors schedule classrooms, laboratories, and shops in a variety of buildings.
10. Vocational directors plan staff in-service activities.

For courses which are descriptive, rather than performance oriented, the instructor organizes explanatory and narrative information with emphasis on time, place, and setting. Historical information, for example, focuses on available sources found in the form of writings, artifacts, and memorabilia. In most instances reputable secondary sources (i.e. reports of people who were not witnesses to the events) suffice as a means for content development. Primary sources (original documents) are preferable for purposes of illustration, comparison, justification, and validation.

In some adult education classes, students participate in determining course objectives. In a welding class, for example, some of the class members may be interested in learning basic bookkeeping procedures for setting up a small business. For those interested in learning industrial welding, the course may be organized differently. Student assessment is necessary to focus course content on adult student priorities.

BEHAVIORAL OBJECTIVES

The use of behavioral objectives for courses and instruction plans is recommended. Behavioral objectives are defined as a means for stating objectives so that observable adult student behaviors are indicated in measurable terms. The primary advantage of behavioral objectives is that they give specific direction for the adult teacher and the adult student. In addition, behavioral objectives:

1. Provide a basis for continuous diagnosis and evaluation
2. Enhance communication between the adult teacher and the adult student
3. Provide a base for systematic program review and development
4. Lend themselves to empirical research
5. Lend themselves to individualized instruction, including programmed instruction
6. Provide a means whereby learning is observable to almost everyone

7. Allow for feedback and measurement of accountability
8. Involve adults in the program and course development process
9. Impose joint adult student and teacher responsibility for learning
10. Encourage adult students to be more efficient in their learning because they know what is expected

Over the past several years, several disadvantages of behavioral objectives have been noted. Behavioral objectives frequently:

1. Restrict content, activity, and methodology
2. Emphasize information which is trivial in nature
3. Are recall oriented and not supportive of creative thinking
4. Emphasize cognitive and psychomotor learning activities and neglect values and attitudes
5. Are time-consuming in terms of preparation
6. Are thought of as unrelated to the broad objectives

The use of behavioral objectives has received wide attention. At the course level of instruction, the content needs to be operationalized. This requires (1) writing behavioral objectives stating content in sentence form to relate what the adult student is to do, and (2) wording the objectives in such a fashion that the adult student must do something which is observable. To be more specific, the steps in writing behavioral objectives are:

Step 1. Use the adult student as the subject of behavioral objectives. The objective should communicate specifically what the adult is expected to do as a result of the learning. Further, objectives written with the adult in mind help to identify appropriate learning activities. Last, the objective describes a change in behavior, and the subject of that behavior change is the adult. In focusing on the adult student, the sought behavior change is consistent with the clientele for whom the objective is intended.

Step 2. Identify and state observable responses expected of the adult student. A behavioral objective describes the task, knowledge, or attitude for which the adult is being trained. For this reason, most behavioral objectives are written in action or doing form. Action verbs are used to help convey activity and accomplishment on the part of the adult. Some of the more commonly used action verbs are:

to adjust	to install	to replenish
to align	to level	to rotate
to analyze	to locate	to route
to ascertain	to lubricate	to salvage
to assemble	to mount	to secure
to balance	to observe	to set up
to calibrate	to overhaul	to signal
to charge	to place	to stow
to connect	to position	to test
to destroy	to program	to tighten
to disassemble	to read	to transport
to disconnect	to receive	to trim
to fabricate	to regulate	to tune
to inspect	to remove	to verify
	to repair	

Unlike such terms as *to be familiar with, to be aware of, to inform,* action verbs are more precise in their meaning and convey a specific type of movement. In the following examples, the behavioral objectives indicate that a task activity is to be accomplished:

The adult student is able to adjust. . .

The adult student is able to locate. . .

The adult student is able to place. . .

The adult student is able to rotate. . .

Step 3. Identify and state tasks as operations to be performed. The objectives specify the learning components of a given task by stating the distinct capabilities or actions needed to perform the particular task. Further, it is important to identify for each capability a body of necessary knowledge, principles, and attitudes, relevant to its successful achievement. Welders, for example, need to know that lighting an arc is dependent not only upon the cylinders being readied, but also upon a desire and willingness to do a good job of welding.

Examples of operations to be performed are:

...the acetylene and oxygen cylinders [placed] in an upright position...

...[cylinders placed] at least four feet from the welding surface...

...the cylinders' (acetylene and oxygen) valves [opened] and then closed quickly in order to discharge dirt materials...

...the twenty-six letters of the alphabet [identified]...

...cake mix, three eggs, four peaches and orange juice [mixed] on low speed until blended...

...a proper round-off flip-flop...

...the alphabet [identified] on an electric typewriter...

...crossword puzzle which provides necessary spaces for the words *adjective, adverb, verb, fable, to,* and *tense*...

Behavioral objectives focus on the adult student, use an action verb, and identify the task to be performed. Sample objectives are as follows:

The adult student is able to position *the acetylene and oxygen cylinders in an upright position at least four feet from the welding surface*...

The adult student is able to recall *the twenty-six letters of the alphabet*...

The adult student is able to construct *a crossword puzzle which provides the necessary spaces for the following words— adjective, adverb, verb, fable, to and tense*...

Step 4.   Identify and state how behavior is to be demonstrated so that learning can be observed. The way in which learned behavior is to be exhibited may not always reflect the exact way the behavior will be used outside the educational setting, but it should approximate as closely as possible the setting eventually used for the performance. A number of terms can be used to describe how the behavior is to be demonstrated. These are:

by connecting lines	by performing
by touching	by demonstrating
by underlining in writing	by speaking
by matching	by pointing
by labeling	by placing in order

In constructing a behavioral objective, the statement should resemble the following:

The adult student is able to position the acetylene and oxygen cylinders in an upright position at least four feet from the welding surface *by demonstrating this ability.*

The adult student is able to recall the twenty-six letters of the alphabet *in written form.*

The adult student is able to do a proper round-off flip-flop without assistance *by performing before the instructor.*

Step 5. Identify and state the standards or quality of outcome desired. The behavioral objective should identify the level that will be used to judge successful performance of the task. The standard of performance should be specific and observable, so that the adult student and teacher can recognize achievement. A few examples of standards include:

within 5 percent accuracy

which meet specifications established by the textbook

so that it has a variance of no more than 10″

according to the adult teacher's specifications

according to building construction codes with perfect construction

in accordance with previously discussed hospital standards

Step 6. Write the behavioral objective in a complete sentence. Once the various components of behavioral objectives are identified, they need to be put together in sentence form. Beginning with a focus on the adult student, the behavioral objective needs to include the desired performance, an active description, the means by which the behavior is to be exhibited, and the criteria for measurement. Completed behavioral objectives are written in the following fashion:

The adult student is able to position the acetylene and oxygen cylinders in an upright position at least four feet from the welding surface by demonstrating the ability according to recommended procedures.

The adult student is able to recall the twenty-six letters of the alphabet in written form with 100 percent accuracy.

The adult student is able to do a proper round-off flip-flop without assistance by performing before the instructor using appropriate techniques.

The adult student is able to construct a crossword puzzle which provides the necessary spaces for the following words— *adjective, adverb, verb, fable, to,* and *tense*—and do so in writing with 90 percent accuracy.

The adult student is able to translate the following sentence into French—"On our way to Copenhagen, we visited our old friends"—and do so in writing with no more than two spelling errors.

The adult student is able to identify without error the four types of concrete blocks by pointing to the appropriate blocks when each type is named.

SELECTED BIBLIOGRAPHY

Akin, J. M. Behavioral objectives in curriculum design: A cautionary note. *The Science Teacher,* 1968, *35* (5), 27-30.

Bailey, S. K. Educational purpose and the pursuit of happiness. *Phi Delta Kappan,* 1976, *58* (1), 42-47.

Baker, R. L., & Gerlach, V. S. *Constructing objectives of cognitive behavior.* New York: Van Nostrand Reinhold Co., 1971.

Benson, C. S., Goldfinger, P. M., Hoachlander, E. G., & Pers, J. S. *Planning for educational reform: Financial and social alternatives.* New York: Dodd, Mead, & Co., 1974.

Bergevin, P., & McKinley, J. *Participation training for adult education.* St. Louis: Bethany Press, 1965.

Burns, R. W. The theory of expressing objectives. *Educational Technology,* 1967, *7* (20), 1-3.

Buser, R. L. *Educational objectives or the objectives of objectives.* Unpublished paper, 1970.

Clark, D. C. *Using instructional objectives in teaching.* Glenview, Illinois: Scott, Foresman & Co., 1972.

Dumas, W. Can we be behaviorists and humanists too? *The Educational Forum,* 1973, *37* (3), 303-306.

Eisner, E. W. Educational objectives: Help or hinderance. *School Review,* 1967, *75* (3), 250-260.

Ganeles, D. Competence-based preparation programs for teachers of adults. *Adult Leadership,* 1974, *23* (6), 187-189.

Illinois State Board of Vocational Education and Rehabilitation, Vocational and Technical Education Division. *Workshop handbook: Writing measurable objectives for career education.* Springfield, Illinois: Author, 1972. (ERIC Document Reproduction Service No. ED 064 502)

Illinois State Board of Vocational Education and Rehabilitation, Vocational and Technical Education Division. *An aid for writing measurable objectives for occupational education.* Springfield, Illinois: Author, 1975.

Kapfer, P. G. Behavioral objectives in the cognitive and affective domains. *Educational Technology,* 1968, *8* (11), 11-13.

Lam, Y. J., & Wong, A. Attendance regularity of adult learners: An examination of content and structural factors. *Adult Education Journal,* 1974, *24* (2), 130-142.

MacDonald, J. B. Myths about instruction. *Educational Leadership,* 1965, *22* (7), 571-576.

Mager, R. F. *Preparing objectives for programmed instruction.* San Francisco: Fearon Publishers, 1961.

Mezirow, J., Darkenwald, G. G., & Knox, A. B. *Last gamble on education.* Washington, D.C.: Adult Education Association of the U.S.A., 1975.

Miller, H. G., & Greer, C. E. Adult education: Performance-based programs. *The Clearing House,* 1973, *48* (2), 121-124.

Nadler, L. *Developing human resources.* Houston, Texas: Gulf Publishing Co., 1970.

Oklahoma State Department of Vocational and Technical Education, Curriculum and Instructional Materials Center. *Behavioral objectives for the teaching-learning process.* Stillwater, Oklahoma: Author, 1971.

Popham, W. J., & Baker, E. L. Note: The instruction objectives preference list. *Journal of Educational Measurement,* 1965, *2* (2), 186.

Williams, R. G., & Miller, H. G. Grading students: A failure to communicate. *The Clearing House,* 1973, *47* (6), 332-337.

7

Organizing Adult
Instructional Plans

Planning for the instructional act is critical for teachers of adults. This chapter reviews planning and organizing for effective teaching, cites two examples of instructional plans, and concludes with examples of learning activities that can be incorporated into instructional plans.

Most adult courses, programs, workshops, or institutes are subdivided for more effective learning. These divisions may take different forms, such as content units, time blocks, textbook chapters, workbook exercises, projects, learning contracts, problem areas, or tutorial sessions. Whatever type of division is used, the instructional units are designed for specific adult learning purposes. They are teaching/learning blueprints illustrating how behavioral objectives are to be achieved.

For most adult teachers, instructional plans provide specific strategies for specific classes. Some adult teachers, however, prefer a tentative unit which applies to several specific class sessions. The type of unit plan and specificity desired depends on the content being taught, the adult teacher's experience in the instructional arena, the performance level expected of the adults in the class, the extent and nature of the behavioral objectives, and the depth and quality in preparation of the total course. In general, as an instructional tool, unit plans:

1. Provide a vehicle for tying content to behavioral objectives
2. Place content in perspective with other instructional responsibilities
3. Emphasize an instructional plan and activity for teacher-directed learning
4. Outline content to be taught
5. Stipulate a succession of teaching activities to maximize the limited instructional time available to most adult education classes

INSTRUCTIONAL PLAN

An instructional plan can be organized in different ways but typically includes sections on behavioral objectives, preassessment and postassessment procedures, content, and activities for instruction as the following basic outline illustrates.

1. BEHAVIORAL OBJECTIVES

The behavioral objectives for an instructional plan need to be clearly written in order to provide effective direction for the rest of the plan. It is assumed that specific and precise objectives will yield accurate and successful instruction. By using the procedures for developing objectives in terms of observable behaviors (as indicated in Chapter Six), both the adult teacher and the adults in class become aware of what is to be achieved and when it has been achieved.

2. PREASSESSMENT OF ENTERING BEHAVIOR

A preassessment is an evaluation of the adult student's knowledge, understanding, and capability in regard to the content to be taught. It is a way to determine whether the adult is ready for instruction and possesses the necessary prerequisites. It also is used to assess an adult's performance level (a criterion measure of capability) and to ascertain the point at which instruction should begin. Based on the behavioral objectives written for the instructional plan, the question remains: "To what extent can the adult achieve the stated objectives?" Individualized adult instruction is based primarily on a preassessment. The preassessment enables the adult teacher to design, modify, and present the content based on the needs and capabilities of the adult students.

Preassessment is like an evaluation or test. It can be given to adults individually or in a group. It can be written or oral or both. In skill areas, competency is best measured by student demonstration and performance. Written preassessment items can be structured or unstructured. Multiple-choice, completion, matching, true-false, essay, and short-answer items are all acceptable if they reflect the behavioral objectives. The advantage of written preassessments, especially when they include multiple-choice and true-false items, is that the items themselves can be validated in terms of test reliability and objectivity. In this sense, error in preassessment item construction can be minimized, and the adult's capability can be more accurately evaluated in relation to the behavioral objectives.

The construction of preassessment instruments based on behavioral objectives should focus on the capabilities to be learned and the behaviors to be exhibited. Depending on the complexity and the content of the instructional plan, the preassessment will vary in length and in time needed for completion. Timed preassessments are appropriate for teaching skills like typing, shorthand, and key punching. In other instructional plans the amount of time required to demonstrate capability may not be an important factor for mastery consideration.

3. CONTENT ORGANIZATION

Organizing content for effective learning is the next critical step in instructional planning. For the most part, behavioral objectives do not specify how content is to be prepared and organized for adult instruction, nor is content sequence inherent in the information to be taught. Most content may be sequenced in a variety of ways depending on individual learning style and instructor priorities. This section presents options for content organization.

Simple-to-Complex Sequence

Arranging content in a hierarchical manner so that progression is from simple to more complex is one form of sequencing. This involves teaching the more elementary aspects of the content before proceeding to the more difficult. The simple-to-complex sequence allows the adult student to use less complex information as a means of transfer to more difficult information. This approach is especially important with adults who are returning to a formalized learning experience and environment after a long period of absence from the classroom. By experiencing initial learning success, adults feel more secure in learning more advanced information. Another reason for a simple-to-complex sequence is that some content requires prior mastery before progression to more difficult information can begin.

The following checklist presents criteria for deciding whether the simple-to-complex sequence is appropriate.

Simple-to-Complex Sequence	Yes	No
1. Would it be helpful to review content already learned and associate this with content yet to be learned?	_____	_____
2. Would it enhance learning to draw a parallel between unknown and known content?	_____	_____

Simple-to-Complex Sequence	Yes	No
3. Are there components of the content which possess fewer or a minimum number of factors, aspects, and tasks?	_____	_____
4. Does an aspect of the content provide a necessary foundation for more advanced content?	_____	_____
5. Does the initial presentation of the content have fewer interrelationships and intricacies?	_____	_____
6. Does the more advanced content require a chaining of actions, skills, and performance?	_____	_____
7. Are some aspects of the content learned and mastered more quickly in terms of time and practice than other aspects?	_____	_____

If the content possesses these or similar characteristics, the simple-to-complex approach should be given serious consideration. Sometimes when content is sequenced in this manner, the complex material represents exceptions and extensions of rules and concepts previously mastered. Frequently, simple content lends itself to more direct practice, measurement, and proficiency.

General-to-Specific Sequence

Another way to sequence information is to arrange the content from general concepts to more specific skills, ideas, and meanings. By establishing the theme, principle, or concept as the starting point in the adult learning experience, the overall program objectives can be emphasized to adults.

A basic advantage of the general-to-specific sequence is that the adult is first introduced to a total view of the content before learning the specifics. Usually such an introduction takes the form of a classification to which adults can relate specific content. A further advantage is that an initial overview enhances retention of specific facts. The overview allows adults to retain a framework for understanding basic concepts without having to memorize a vast amount of separate items. Likewise, adults are better able to internalize the content under study because they have a long-term map of how the content evolves.

The general-to-specific sequencing can be used in various ways. In deciding whether this method is appropriate, the instructor can ask the following questions.

General-to-Specific Sequence	Yes	No
1. Can specific information be used as examples to illustrate commonality and an overall classification?		
2. Is there an apparent grouping of content by common characteristics?		
3. Can emphasis be based upon related similarities?		
4. Are the classifications and divisions more important than specific factual information?		
5. Can the classifications be used by the adults in the course?		
6. Will further learning plans and courses be devoted to more specific information?		

If the answers to the above questions are yes, then the general-to-specific sequence is probably a useful way to structure content for a learning segment.

Concrete-to-Abstract Sequence

An effective way of structuring content for use by adults who are unfamiliar with the content or who are experiencing some difficulty with certain aspects is to organize the material in a concrete-to-abstract sequence. Adults can often learn more effectively when they are able to learn concrete-manipulative content first. Involving adults in actual physical observations and manipulations provides a basis for more abstract and symbolic concept learning.

Several advantages are inherent in the use of the concrete-to-abstract approach of sequencing content. First, a concrete learning experience tends to be more sensory oriented; seeing, touching, tasting, and hearing are involved. Second, the use of concrete, visible models as examples provides adults with an available reference point for the more complex, abstract material when needed. Third, when adults who lack the vocabulary, word associations, and thinking skills to grasp abstract ideas can view and work with the situation in a concrete fashion, they are more likely to be successful in the learning experience.

To determine if the content is amenable to a concrete-to-abstract sequencing approach, consider the following criteria.

Concrete-to-Abstract Sequence	Yes	No
1. Does the content possess abstractions or rules which need to be taught?		
2. Does the content lend itself to the use of concrete-manipulative learning?		
3. Are the abstractions and rules clearly stated and identified?		
4. Do abstractions provide a higher or more complex level of understanding?		
5. Are symbolism and abbreviations common features of the content?		

Chronological Sequence

Relating content in terms of time, fixed periods, and dates in order of occurrence is yet another sequencing approach. It is a means of illustrating the successive relationships of one event to another. Usually chronology refers to arranging information which may be either of a more immediate or of a more remote nature. Chronology is not restricted to arranging the past but may also be used for arranging proposed events and activities. A unique feature of chronology is its potential for conveying a cause-and-effect relationship.

There are several advantages in using chronology as a means of content sequencing. Foremost, it is an easy form to use. Frequently, it is simply a matter of noting which events, activities, or places happened first, second, or third. It is a form that is used frequently and one which most people are accustomed to. A chronological arrangement assists in identifying patterns, commonalities, and consistencies. From these patterns, probability can be assessed, and predictions can be made. By knowing and studying what has gone on before, a point of reference can be established for making comparisons and evaluations.

Criteria for using chronology are found in the following questions.

Chronological Sequence	Yes	No
1. Does the content emphasize time, fixed periods, and events?		
2. Does a progression of information need to be presented?		
3. Do events, activities, or places need to be noted?		
4. Is there background information (providing a context) to be taught?		

Chronological Sequence	Yes	No
5. Do trends, patterns, commonalities, and consistencies need to be illustrated?	_____	_____

If the answer to all the above questions is yes, a chronological sequence is appropriate. A limitation of chronology is that it is difficult to use when there is a great deal of information to be explained in a very short time span.

4. LEARNING ACTIVITIES

With the content determined and outlined, an instructor next decides upon and develops the many possible learning activities to be used. Simulations, drill exercises (see Chapter Eight), overhead transparencies, illustrations, and anecdotes also need to be included in the instructional unit plan. Sample learning activities are provided at the end of this chapter.

Special attention should be given to making assignments when developing learning activities for an instructional unit. Some of the more common reasons for using assignments in adult instruction are that they individualize instruction, they assist in achieving the behavioral objectives of the unit, and they provide information on an adult's achievement. Types of assignments commonly incorporated include: supplemental and textbook readings; class presentations, such as reports and panels; workbook exercises; programmed instruction; media aids, such as films, filmstrips, and recordings; written reports and papers; and the design and construction of special projects, models, and forms.

In making assignments, adults should be given both written and verbal instructions about what should be done, why it should be done, how it is to be done, and when it is to be done. In those assignments that involve skill learning, the teacher should provide a demonstration and opportunities for modeling behavior so that adult practice can be effective.

Some suggestions for making assignments are presented in the list below and provide good criteria for measuring the worth of the assignments.

Suggestions for Making Assignments	Yes	No
1. Are resources for doing the assignment readily available to adults?		
2. Are assignments made far enough in advance for adequate completion?		
3. Are assignments designed for the individual adult's learning needs?		
4. Are assignments designed to be consistent with the behavioral objectives of the instructional plan?		
5. Are assignments designed to provide specific feedback to adults?		
6. Are adult students involved in making decisions about assignments?		
7. Are assignments made with consideration given to the time that adults have available for doing the work?		

5. POSTASSESSMENT

Postassessment, like preassessment, is the process of determining the extent to which the behavioral objectives have been achieved. It is an evaluation of what learning has occurred following instruction. The same general procedures used for preassessment should be followed. Chapter Nine deals with evaluation procedures and the construction of tests for instructional plans and provides an in-depth review of evaluation procedures applicable to preassessment and postassessment.

The degree of mastery expected by the adult teacher and the adult student is one consideration in determining the amount of effort and time required for learning. In some instances, minimum understanding is acceptable, while in other instances a highly sophisticated degree of performance is expected. Understandably, the level of performance needed affects the amount of time and type of instruction to be used. Generally, the more complex the content is, the more important it is to have instructional plans that emphasize specific performance. Lacking this, there is a tendency to spend an equal amount of instructional time without differentiating between content difficulty and learning needs.

CONSTRUCTING INSTRUCTIONAL PLANS

Once content is organized and sequenced for effective learning, an instructional plan should be designed which includes the above components. Learning is achieving—not so much by enlightenment as by an accumulation and mastering of information. Effective instruction needs to be planned and executed in terms of learnable segments. To divide content into acceptable learning segments, several factors should be taken into consideration.

The type of content to be taught and the adults' performance level at the outset of the class affect how a course or plan is to be taught. Skill-oriented content may require extra time for tutorial teaching and practice. Adult students will also need time to view demonstrations and to model and rehearse the desired skills. The more skill-oriented the content, the more carefully the adult needs to be assessed so that instruction can be directed at an appropriate level.

Another aspect to be considered in designing learning units is the frequency of instruction and the amount of time available.

Adult teachers need to adjust their teaching to a schedule that has been developed for specific learning needs. The fact that instructional time is frequently provided based on set learning periods and availability of learning centers does not necessarily mean that an effective learning schedule has been designed and is being implemented. Furthermore, the availability of instructional time is not always an aspect of instruction which can be altered to fit the learning needs.

It is a commonly accepted principle that frequent instruction and practice within reasonable intervals are more effective than infrequent instruction or instruction that is provided on a limited basis and offered at irregular intervals. It is better, for example, to have twenty minutes of instruction every day than an hour of instruction every two weeks. Generally, if learning periods are too long, fatigue, distraction, and poor concentration will limit performance. Frequent instruction is important for increasing adult proficiency. Once a satisfactory level has been achieved, a learning schedule should be provided that maintains what has been learned for use in mastering new content. Continuous practice and frequent proficiency measurement are the best means to assure high level performance. On the other hand, unnecessarily occupying instructional time is just as inappropriate as attempting to teach too much information or demanding a higher level of performance than time will permit.

Once the type of sequencing is determined, the teacher outlines the content for presentation. The content outline can take the typical format—items in phrase or sentence form arranged with major points listed before less important information. Another way to organize instructional units is an essay format composed of either short statements or paragraphs. Sometimes side headings or paragraph headings similar to those in most textbooks are used to reflect major emphasis.

Whatever outline format is used, it should be easy to construct, it should reflect the order in which the content is to be taught, and it should be convenient to teach from. The approach used should further emphasize the basic concepts, facts, and understandings that will be presented. These emphases should reflect the behavioral objectives which have been written for the instructional plan.

Utilizing the above-mentioned ideas on developing instructional plans would result in a coordinated statement for teaching adults. Two examples illustrating this planning technique follow.

INSTRUCTIONAL PLAN ON MEASURING THE LENGTH OF STEEL PIPE FOR INSTALLATION

1. *Behavioral Objective*
The adult student at the end of instruction will be able to measure a section of running pipe in feet and inches to allow for fitting gain and makeup by demonstrating the ability and computing the answer.
2. *Preassessment*
    2.1. A fitting gain is the amount of space
        a. taken up by the fitting into which the pipe is screwed
        b. left over by the fitting when using drainage fittings
        c. allowed for by a steel pipe and fitting for clearance between interior walls
        d. determined to be appropriate for standard fittings as opposed to drainage fittings when measuring a drain-waste-vent system of a two-story house
        e. none of the above
    2.2. Generally, how many different ways can steel pipes be measured?
        a. One
        b. Two
        c. Three
        d. Four
    2.3. Threaded steel pipe fittings are standardized.
        a. True
        b. False

2.4. Makeup in a fitting is the amount of space
   a. taken up by the pipe when put into a fitting
   b. allowed for by the width of the pipe for determining dimension of a fitting
   c. when multiplied by the width and the length determines the volume
   d. present within the pipe

2.5. Fitting gain and makeup should be considered for assembling steel pipes.
   a. True
   b. False

2.6. Plumbing pipes are generally made of _____ types of materials.
   a. Two
   b. Three
   c. Four
   d. Five

2.7. Suppose you want to connect a ½-inch steel pipe between two existing pipe fittings for a distance of 40 inches. One fitting connection is a tee branch, and the other is a 90° elbow. How many inches of pipe are actually needed?
   a. 36¾ inches
   b. 35¾ inches
   c. 34¾ inches
   d. 37¾ inches

3. *Content Outline*
   I. Three types of pipes—Advantages
      A. Galvanized steel
         1. Strong, therefore takes much abuse
            a. Good for installing under roadways
            b. Withstands strong water pressures
         2. Standardized and has been used for many years
      B. Copper
         1. Very resistant to corrosion
         2. Strong solder fittings

    3. Easy to install
    4. Requires fewer fittings because of flexibility
   C. Plastic
    1. Low cost in comparison to steel and copper
    2. Smooth interior and thus less friction
    3. Solvent welding—quick, less messy, and easy to
        work with
 II. Measuring a steel pipe done in three ways
   A. End to end of connecting pipes
   B. End of pipe to center of fitting
   C. Center of fitting to center of fitting
III. For most cases, standardized fittings available
   A. Examples of some standardized fittings
    1. Elbow
    2. Tee Branch
    3. Coupling
    4. Reducer
    5. 45° Elbow
    6. Street L
   B. Space allowances for standard fittings

Pipe Size	Distance	Elbow	Tee	Reducer
1/2 in.	1/2 in.	1 1/8 in.	1 1/8 in.	1 1/4 in.
3/4 in.	1/2 in.	1 5/16 in.	1 5/16 in.	1 7/16 in.
1 in.	9/16 in.	1 1/2 in.	1 1/2 in.	1 11/16 in.

 IV. Fitting gain—the amount of space taken up by the fitting
      which the pipe is screwed into
  V. Fitting makeup—the amount of space taken up by the
      pipe when put into a fitting
 VI. Method of determining the length of steel pipe needed
      between two fittings
   A. Determine the amount of space the fittings will take
       (use table)
   B. Measure from center to center of existing fittings
   C. Subtract fittings from center to center measurement
   D. Add distance and arrive at the final answer

4. *Assignment*
  4.1. Please read *Plumbing Techniques and Standards,* pp. 342-370.
5. *Postassessment*
  5.1. Most steel fittings for steel pipes are standardized.
      a. True
      b. False
  5.2. List the three most common types of pipes.
      a. _____
      b. _____
      c. _____
  5.3. A fitting makeup is the amount of space taken up by the pipe when put into a fitting.
      a. True
      b. False
  5.4. A fitting gain is the amount of space or clearance allowed between interior walls for a steel pipe and fitting.
      a. True
      b. False
  5.5. Suppose you want to connect a 1-inch steel pipe between a Tee and Reducer. The distance from center to center of the fittings is 20 inches. How many inches of pipe are actually needed?

INSTRUCTIONAL PLAN ON NATIONHOOD FOR AN ADULT BASIC EDUCATION PROGRAM

1. *Behavioral Objective*
The adult student can identify six characteristics of a country by being able to list and describe these characteristics on a piece of paper.
2. *Preassessment*
  2.1. Some countries in recent times are developing their own language or reviving their ancient language. Identify

those countries from the list below:
a. Canada
b. Iran
c. Israel
d. Ireland
e. France

2.2. Finland, Belgium, and Switzerland each has:
a. a common geographical border
b. more than one official state language
c. a state church
d. all of the above

2.3. List six characteristics that make up a country.

3. *Content Outline*
What are some basic characteristics that make up a country?

    A. Government
       1. Forms of government
         a. Dictatorship
         b. Representative democracy
         c. Monarchy
       2. American political parties
         a. Voluntary association and relationship among voters
         b. Republican and Democratic parties
    B. Language
       1. One official language per country
       2. Language denotes the name of people
         a. Swedish
         b. Russian
         c. French
         d. German
       3. Language common to several countries
         a. English—Canada, New Zealand, Australia, United States
         b. Common/shared history

    4. More than one official language
       a. Finland
       b. Belgium
       c. Switzerland
    5. Countries developing a language to help create tradition
       a. Ireland—Gaelic
       b. Israel—Hebrew

C. Geography
    1. Natural boundaries
       a. Rivers
       b. Mountains
       c. Oceans
       d. Lakes
       e. Deserts
    2. Man-made barriers
       a. Great Wall of China
       b. Berlin Wall
       c. Iron Curtain

D. Common history
    1. Political history
    2. National holidays and festivals
    3. Wars ·
    4. Great men and women

E. Religion
    1. Church states
    2. Does not respect national boundaries

F. Economic system
    1. Types of economies
       a. Farming
       b. Industries
       c. Technology
    2. Economic indicators
       a. GNP
       b. Supply and demand

4. *Assignments*
   4.1. Wordsearch Puzzle
      Circle the following words in the puzzle:
      1. Government
      2. Language
      3. Geography
      4. History
      5. Religion
      6. Economy
      7. Country
      8. Population
      9. Boundary
      10. Culture

D	K	E	A	H	E	P	F	I	G	C	A	I	E	O
H	J	L	S	I	A	L	U	Q	N	O	V	L	D	T
R	O	W	G	S	V	X	D	C	U	L	T	U	R	E
A	T	F	L	T	K	E	J	O	T	N	J	R	S	K
Q	P	I	K	O	H	A	Z	U	Q	F	C	B	E	P
G	O	V	E	R	N	M	E	N	T	H	A	M	C	E
E	P	M	T	Y	B	C	R	T	G	U	I	T	O	G
C	U	U	X	G	L	T	Z	R	M	D	H	N	N	K
H	L	N	D	W	A	B	H	Y	E	Q	J	C	O	B
D	A	G	U	I	N	G	L	O	E	N	B	P	M	F
J	T	F	S	K	G	E	O	G	R	A	P	H	Y	H
O	I	M	H	E	U	C	D	V	W	G	L	X	U	I
B	O	U	N	D	A	R	Y	H	A	M	C	Q	E	E
D	N	Z	W	M	G	K	J	I	S	U	Y	L	O	E
B	C	L	H	R	E	L	I	G	I	O	N	T	Z	I

4.2. Directions: Some of the characteristics of a nation are listed below. Circle the number that you feel best indicates the importance of each characteristic in the formation of a country. A zero (0) would mean that the characteristic is unimportant, while a five (5) would suggest that it is quite important.

Common Religion	0	1	2	3	4	5
Democracy	0	1	2	3	4	5
Common Language	0	1	2	3	4	5
Geographical Boundaries	0	1	2	3	4	5
Farming Economy	0	1	2	3	4	5
News	0	1	2	3	4	5
Historical Ties	0	1	2	3	4	5
Money	0	1	2	3	4	5
Law	0	1	2	3	4	5
Educational System	0	1	2	3	4	5
Socialism	0	1	2	3	4	5

4.3. Assume that a country has just been formed. It is an island with a population of one million people. The economy of the country is farming. The capital is located in the middle of the island. A prime minister is the head of the government and head of the church. From this description, draw a flag for this country.

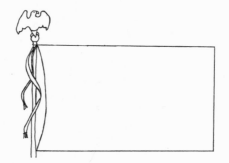

4.4. Discuss the following passage: "It is odd, but for some reason the phrase, 'The United States,' is on the lips of everyone. Somehow the farmer of the west, the Southern planter, and the merchant of the east have begun to believe that we are no longer the children of England. Instead, we are men, free and independent, who should stand alone. From whence has this belief come? What does it mean?"

From the diary of a Boston merchant
June 3, 1772

4.5. Match the characteristics in the right hand column with the nations in the left hand column. Place the correct letter in the left hand column in front of the name of the country.

_____1. China	a. surrounded by water
_____2. Britain	b. Hebrew
_____3. Finland	c. Great Wall
_____4. Canada & New	
Zealand	d. a barter economy
_____5. Switzerland	e. two official languages
	f. English speaking
	g. surrounded by mountains
	h. oil

5. *Postassessment*

5.1. List the six characteristics of a country.

a. _____

b. _____

c. _____

d. _____

e. _____

f. _____

5.2. Ireland and France are developing or reviving their ancient languages as a means to enhance nationhood.

a. True

b. False

5.3.   Finland, Belgium, and Switzerland have more than one
       official language.
       a.   True
       b.   False
5.4.   Natural boundaries would include:
       a.   Rivers
       b.   Great Wall of China
       c.   International time zone
       d.   Rock formations

SELECTED LEARNING ACTIVITIES

When preparing an instructional plan for adults, the teacher
should also develop learning activities. These can be done either
individually in a class setting or given as an assignment. Since most
adults tend to be very task and achievement oriented, learning
activities that can be completed in a short period of time, that
provide positive feedback, and that can be done individually are
useful. A further reason for using learning activities is that adults
tend to be more successful when learning through participation.
A problem situation calls for adults to demonstrate their understanding and ability. Possible learning activities for use in adult
instruction are described in this section.

Crossword Puzzle

Working a crossword puzzle not only reinforces word-association
skills but also provides reinforcement of concepts and terms.
Crossword puzzles are a common technique for problem solving
often found in newspapers and magazines. Crossword puzzles
generally require completion-type responses. The procedures for
constructing a crossword puzzle are: (1) selecting a topic or
subject, (2) obtaining information about the topic and noting
those statements with one or two key words, (3) selecting the
longest word as the base word, (4) writing the base word on a sheet
of paper either vertically or horizontally, (5) trying to fit the rest

of the words to the base word or to a word already attached to the base word, (6) writing a statement (as a clue) for the words that have been used, (7) numbering the words and the statements, and (8) drawing a crossword box providing the necessary spaces for the identified words.

Examples of Crossword Puzzles

Example #1

COMPOSITION AND GRAMMAR

Adjective—modifies and describes nouns
Adverb—ends in *ly:* where, when, and how
Auxiliary Verb—be, have, and do
Fable—story with animals as characters
To—infinitive
Tense—indicates time

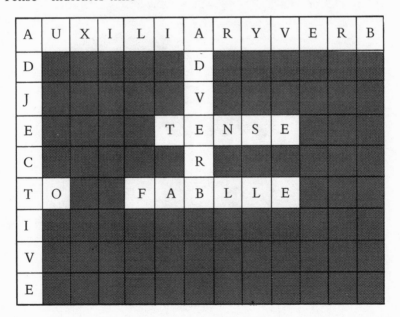

A	U	X	I	L	I	A	R	Y	V	E	R	B
D						D						
J						V						
E				T	E	N	S	E				
C						R						
T	O			F	A	B	L	L	E			
I												
V												
E												

Example #2

MATHEMATICS

Volume—closed surface
Triangle—union of three lines at an angle
Union—set of all elements
Symmetrical—of equal proportions
Power—exponent of the base number

										T
										R
		V								I
	P	O	W	E	R					A
		L					U			N
		U					N			G
S	Y	M	M	E	T	R	I	C	A	L
		E					O			E
							N			

Wordsearch Puzzle

A wordsearch puzzle is constructed in the same fashion as the crossword puzzle except that all of the blanks in a puzzle have letters. The adult is given the word or phrase and asked to find the word among a mixture of letters. More difficult wordsearch puzzles place the words on a diagonal, spell words backward, and spell words from left to right. Also more words may be listed than are provided in the puzzle. This adds more difficulty to the exercise. As with crossword puzzles, one purpose of wordsearch puzzles is to reinforce word associations and correct spelling. To construct a wordsearch puzzle, select the words to be used, choose the longest word, and place it in a crossword box either horizontally, vertically, or diagonally. Add the remaining words to the box using the letters of the word already placed. The words can be connected to other words or can be separate; they can be spelled upside down, backward, or diagonally. The last step is to fill the spaces not used with random letters from the alphabet.

Examples of Wordsearch Puzzles

Example #1

ASTRONOMY

Circle the names of the following planets:

Mercury	Jupiter
Venus	Uranus
Mars	Neptune

								S
J	U	P	I	T	E	R	Y	U
					N	R		N
			M		U			E
			A	C	T			V
			R		P			
		E	S		E			
	M		S	U	N	A	R	U

A	I	L	J	U	V	G	S	S
J	U	P	I	T	E	R	Y	U
B	H	K	W	K	N	R	T	N
N	O	G	M	X	U	L	Y	E
D	U	U	A	C	T	R	Z	V
E	X	W	R	M	P	Q	A	Q
Z	O	E	S	N	E	O	S	T
X	M	P	S	U	N	A	R	U

Example #2

NURSING CARE

Circle the following first aid terms:

Tourniquet	Concussion
Closed Fracture	Skull Fracture
Open Fracture	Shock
Splints	Unconsciousness
Dislocations	

E	R	U	T	C	A	R	F		D	E	S	O	L	C
F	R	A	C	T	U	R	E		O	P	E	N		U
				N								N		
					O					C				
D						I				O				
I							S		N					
S			S	P	L	I	N	T	S					
L			H				C		U					
O			O			I				C				
C			C			O					N			
A			K		U								O	
T				S										C
I				N										
O		E												
N	S	K	U	L	L	F	R	A	C	T	U	R	E	
S		T	O	U	R	N	I	Q	U	E	T			

E	R	U	T	C	A	R	F	W	D	E	S	O	L	C
F	R	A	C	T	U	R	E	K	O	P	E	N	Q	U
A	U	I	F	H	N	K	W	L	S	W	G	O	N	B
I	F	Q	H	V	G	O	P	Q	F	J	R	C	E	U
D	X	X	M	B	L	Y	I	R	G	G	O	Z	O	F
I	C	L	C	E	Z	M	K	S	K	N	A	E	X	T
S	N	B	S	P	L	I	N	T	S	E	Y	J	A	O
L	X	U	H	T	M	P	R	C	T	U	Y	E	S	I
O	R	C	O	D	C	S	I	N	Z	Z	C	F	M	U
C	V	B	C	J	L	O	S	X	Y	N	R	N	H	H
A	K	P	K	W	U	W	Z	C	D	L	B	Y	O	A
T	E	B	V	S	K	N	N	U	D	H	L	O	C	C
I	I	T	N	A	F	P	G	V	U	S	T	Q	G	O
O	Q	E	J	D	A	F	R	V	I	E	W	Z	D	D
N	S	K	U	L	L	F	R	A	C	T	U	R	E	P
S	J	T	O	U	R	N	I	Q	U	E	T	K	M	O

Word Scramble Puzzle

By using terms, names, or descriptions and mixing the letters of the words, the adult is asked to unscramble each word and write the correct spelling on a line. This type of learning activity is good practice for vocabulary development and spelling accuracy. Letters of a word can be scrambled at random, or the word can be spelled backward. Sometimes when a word has several of the same letters, these letters can be grouped together. Generally, there are no clues given as to the correct spelling of the word other than the letters in the scramble. A variation is to solve the puzzle with books open or to provide a list of the scrambled words and unscrambled words and to have adults match the two lists.

Examples of Word Scramble Puzzles

Example #1

TYPING

Listed below are various parts of the typewriter. You are to unscramble each word and write the correct spelling on the line provided to the right of the scrambled word.

BERKAYOD   _____

MWOHERO   _____

LESEERPAPAER   _____

MARMHTIGRGI   _____

PRABIPLEA   _____

GEMFALRTNI   _____

BATTES   _____

NGIRRLEEAMEAS   _____

Example #2

MUSIC

Provided are a list of scrambled and unscrambled titles of band method books. Match the two lists.

_____1. drahfiondeitosdnmivbist   a. Belwin Elementary Band Method

_____2. danbrofdohtemretsam   b. Belwin Intermediate Band Method

_____3. nelbiw meeeiniatdtr badn tdohem   c. First Division Band Method

_____4. dldoblemarahoeanndhe ttemnaryel   d. Master Method for Band

_____5. eeeeebbnnnttoaawmm illddryh   e. Hal Leonard Elementary Band Method

Cryptogram Puzzle

A cryptogram is a form of writing code in which each letter of the alphabet is replaced by another letter. For example, the letter *a* is replaced with letter *e*; the letter *e* is replaced each time with the letter *z*. This process is continued until the entire alphabet has been coded. In some instances, figures or symbols are used for the code instead of replaced alphabet letters. Cryptograms can be used with phrases, statements, terms, and quotations. They reinforce vocabulary and recall development and at the same time encourage adults to work with the alphabet.

Examples of Cryptogram Puzzles

Example #1

ADULT LEARNING

Decipher this basic principle of adult instruction.

MVOO   EV,   X   HTSAVM;
WBTD   EV,   X   SVEVEPVS;
XUJTOJV   EV,   X   YUGVSWMKUG.

Solution:
Tell me, I forget;
Show me, I remember;
Involve me, I understand.

Example #2

POWER TOOLS

Decipher the names of these power tools.

IZWRZO   ZIN   HZD
HGZGRLMZIBKLDVIHZD
ULFI—HKVVW   TZK   YVW   OZGSV
IZWROZO   WIROO   KIVHH

Solution:
   Radial Arm Saw
   Stationary Power Saw
   Four-Speed Gap Bed Lathe
   Radial Drill Press

Missing Letter Search

A missing letter search is like a completion exercise. The adult is given a term, phrase, or statement that is written with letters missing. The goal is to complete missing word items accurately from a pool of letters provided. The pool of letters can have the exact number of letters needed or can include additional letters. In some missing letter searches, a statement similar to crossword puzzles is given as a clue for the term and the missing letters. Pictures and word completions are also used as a means of completing a sentence or term. This type of technique, which has several variations, can provide practice and reinforcement for spelling, vocabulary development, and word awareness.

Examples of Missing Letter Search Puzzles

Example #1

CONSUMER EDUCATION

Using letters from the pool provided, accurately complete the spelling of the following consumer education terms. Each letter in the pool may be used only once.

ABCDEFGHIJKLMNOPQRSTUVWXYZZYXWVUTSR
QPONMLKJIHGFEDCBAAEIOUYTSQBEMZWXYZRO
PFJJXZABCDEFGHIJKLMNOPQRSTUVWXYZOLBD
FHIJKYWUTRQOMNIEFAEACBFINSSTONMRGGEU

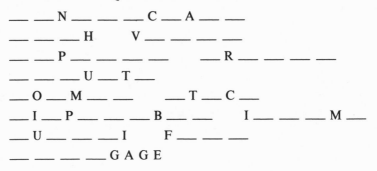

_ _ N _ _ _ C _ A _ _

_ _ _ H   V _ _ _ _

_ _ P _ _ _ _   _ R _ _ _ _

_ _ _ U _ T _

_ O _ M _ _   _ T _ C _

_ I _ P _ _ _ B _ _   I _ _ _ M _

_ U _ _ _ I   F _ _ _

_ _ _ _ G A G E

Example #2

SECRETARIAL SKILLS

Listed below are terms used in the secretarial business program. Using the clues provided, find the missing letters and complete each term.

Descriptions:
1. A brief business message
2. A receipt of purchase
3. A statement of assets and liabilities

4. Monthly accounting of receipts
5. Cash and other assets to be received

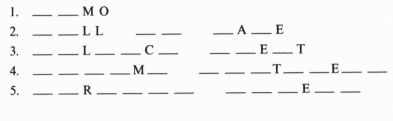

AAAAAABBCCCCEEEEEEEEEEFHIIIIILLMMMMNNN
NNNNOOOORRSSSSSSSSTTTTTTU

1. ___ ___ M O
2. ___ ___ L L   ___ ___   ___ A ___ E
3. ___ ___ L ___ ___ C ___   ___ ___ E ___ T
4. ___ ___ ___ ___ M ___   ___ ___ ___ T ___ ___ E ___ ___
5. ___ ___ R ___ ___ ___ ___ ___   ___ ___ ___ E ___ ___

Rank-Order Technique

The rank-order technique is one in which adults are asked to rearrange ·a list of items according to their own preference from most desirable or significant to least desirable or insignificant. This technique can be varied by having adults select the three most significant items or the three least ·significant items from a given list. Frequently, items are accompanied by a brief description so that adults consider specific factors about each item in their selection. By having adults make selections on the basis of their own criteria (how they feel about the items), the adult teacher is focusing on individual reactions and values for discussion, clarification, and reevaluation.

Examples of Rank-Order Techniques

Example #1

GREAT ADVANCES IN SCIENCE

Because of great scientific discoveries and advances in the twentieth century, the world probably has changed more in the last seventy-two years than it did in over four thousand years before this. Can you imagine what kind of response you would get if you could go back to the year 1900 and tried to describe a television set to someone?

Suppose that you were on an evaluation committee to determine which scientific developments would be presented on a nationwide television program entitled "THE GREATEST SCIENTIFIC DEVELOPMENTS OF THE 20TH CENTURY." You would have to decide which four of the following developments have benefited mankind most in the twentieth century and then rank the four according to their importance. How would you do it?

A. *Internal-Combustion Engine*—Although the internal-combustion engine was developed at the end of the eighteenth century, it did not become practical until the early 1900s. Today, there are over seventy million automobiles in the United States alone, providing widespread transportation to nearly every member of our society. On the other hand, thousands of people die each year in auto accidents, exhaust pollution is becoming a major problem, and the American people spend millions of working hours each year in order to pay for expensive cars.

B. *Space Travel*—Space travel and exploration have come about only in the last twenty years. Today we have television satellites continually circling the earth bringing us on-the-spot television reception from the other side of the globe. Weather satellites are very useful in reporting cloud buildups and other weather developments from all over the world. Many people say the United States is spending too much money on space travel and research. They contend that this money could be put to better use in rebuilding American urban centers.

C. *Improved Plant Breeding*—Through the study of genetics, many new and extremely important plant varieties have been developed. Today, because of improvements in such plants as wheat, corn, and rice, the people of the world have a much better diet than would have been possible with the old system of agriculture. Even with this tremendous improvement, most of the people in the world are still undernourished because the population seems to grow as fast or faster than improvements can be made.

D. *Consumer Electricity*—Although electricity was discovered about two hundred years ago, it did not come into popular use until approximately fifty years ago. In many rural areas in the United States, it has not been available until very recently. Most areas of the world are still not adequately supplied with electricity. Electricity pollutes our environment to some extent. Air pollution is created by burning fossil fuels, such as coal, to produce electricity. Every year more land is flooded when new hydroelectric dams are constructed.

E. *Penicillin*—Penicillin is one of the most useful drugs known to man. It was first used during World War II to save the lives of thousands of wounded soldiers. Since then, it has been found that penicillin is an effective cure for such diseases as pneumonia, gas gangrene, scarlet fever, syphilis, meningitis, endocarditis, and rheumatic fever. Scientists presently are concerned that many of the bacterial strains that are killed by penicillin may become resistant and unaffected by it in the future.

F. *Nuclear Bomb*—It is commonly believed that the atomic bombing of two Japanese cities near the end of World War II actually resulted in an earlier end to the war than would have normally occurred, thus saving the lives of many people who would have been killed if the war had continued. Some people also believe that the presence of nuclear bombs will prevent another all-out destruction.

G. *Atomic Energy*—Atomic energy is a clean, relatively nonpolluting, and economical source of energy. Presently, it is used to produce a small percentage of our electricity and to power a number of ships and submarines. In the future it will probably become one of our main sources of energy, thus decreasing the total amount of pollution in our environment.

Example #2

AMERICAN HISTORY

Rearrange the following historical events in order of importance to you.

_____1. 1492—Columbus's discovery of the New World
_____2. 1620—Mayflower Compact
_____3. 1775—The American Revolution
_____4. 1783-1789—The Critical Period
_____5. 1787—The Northwest Ordinance
_____6. 1790s—XYZ Affair

Extrapolation Technique

The extrapolation technique is another way to encourage and initiate class discussion. Adults are given a list of words or phrases that are more or less relevant to a given topic, such as a list of words that characterize a given culture or society. Adults are asked to select the terms that best or least describe the topic. Also, the adult teacher could ask adult students to select those words from a list that best describe and exemplify a topic or theme. This technique is good for exploring and clarifying stereotypes and generalizations.

Examples of Extrapolation Techniques

Example #1

SECRETARIAL OFFICE SKILLS

Circle those words in the following list that, in your opinion, best describe an office secretary.

1. A woman
2. A man
3. A woman over 40
4. A woman under 30
5. A person who mainly types
6. A person who mainly files
7. A person who compiles statistics
8. A person who keeps budgets
9. A person who has a private office
10. A person who earns $25,000 a year
11. A person who travels

Example #2

GERMAN

Circle those German terms that, in your opinion, best describe German society today.

1. glücklich (happy)
2. religiös (religious)
3. weiblich (feminine)
4. faul (lazy)
5. stark (strong)
6. langweilig (boring)
7. pünktlich (punctual)
8. ernst (serious)
9. reizend (charming)
10. duldsam (tolerant)

Differential Technique

The differential technique asks adults to choose between two opposing descriptors with regard to a particular topic, theme, event, or happening. It encourages adults to express their attitudes and acts as a good discussion-starter. A variation of the technique is to ask the adults to respond as they think another person, family member, or relative would respond to the items. In this way, a comparison can be made between how the adult responds and how the adult believes another person would respond to the same item.

Examples of Differential Techniques

Example #1

TODAY'S WORLD OF JOURNALISM

For each set of opposing terms, check the space that indicates how you feel about journalism.
1. accurate ___ ___ ___ or ___ ___ ___ inaccurate
2. sensational ___ ___ ___ or ___ ___ ___ dull
3. too probing ___ ___ ___ or ___ ___ ___ too restrained
4. responsible ___ ___ ___ or ___ ___ ___ irresponsible
5. entertaining ___ ___ ___ or ___ ___ ___ boring
6. valuable ___ ___ ___ or ___ ___ ___ a waste
7. fair ___ ___ ___ or ___ ___ ___ unfair
8. helpful ___ ___ ___ or ___ ___ ___ useless
9. infallible ___ ___ ___ or ___ ___ ___ fallible
10. humanitarian ___ ___ ___ or ___ ___ ___ nonhuman
11. reports the news ___ ___ ___ or ___ ___ ___ creates the news

Example #2

THE CONCEPT OF WORK

For each set of opposing terms, check the space indicating how you feel about work. Then do the same thing again except check the space indicating how you think a bank president feels about work.

Yourself

good ___ ___ or ___ ___ bad
pleasant ___ ___ or ___ ___ unpleasant
easy ___ ___ or ___ ___ hard
important ___ ___ or ___ ___ unimportant
useful ___ ___ or ___ ___ useless
practical ___ ___ or ___ ___ theoretical
physical ___ ___ or ___ ___ mental
rewarding ___ ___ or ___ ___ unrewarding
work few hours ___ ___ or ___ ___ work many hours

Should/Should Not—Is/Is Not Technique

In this technique, a list of descriptors, activities, characteristics, or terms are provided; and adults are asked to decide whether the item should or should not be applied. An "is/is not" format is sometimes used when perceptions of an actual activity are being sought. Both "should/should not" and "is/is not" can be used to compare a current perception with a preference for what should or should not be.

Examples of Should/Should Not—Is/Is Not Techniques

Example #1

GIVING A SPEECH

The following are possible activities when preparing for and giving a persuasive speech. Check the appropriate space as to whether you feel a speaker should or should not engage in the described practice.

Should   **Should Not**

_____ 1. Copy your speech word for word from _____
your sources

_____ 2. Avoid using any notes   _____

_____ 3. Memorize all notes   _____

_____ 4. Say "quote" and "unquote"   _____

_____ 5. Use clichés and stories to make points _____

_____ 6. Apologize if you make a mistake   _____

Example #2

HOW ADULTS LEARN

The following items describe ways that adults learn. Check the spaces that in your opinion are appropriate. Not all spaces will be marked.

Is	Should	Items	Is Not	Should Not
—	—	Visually Based	—	—
—	—	Content Centered	—	—
—	—	Task Achievement Oriented	—	—
—	—	Aural Learning	—	—
—	—	Book Oriented	—	—
—	—	Active Involvement	—	—
—	—	Concept Oriented	—	—
—	—	Object Oriented	—	—

PREPARATION REMINDERS

In preparing for an adult class, the teacher needs to remember a variety of factors. First, the learning environment of the classroom is important and should not be overlooked. Coat racks, nearby restrooms, ash trays, available parking, comfortable seats, good ventilation, coffee and other refreshments, and good lighting are all important to the success of an adult learning experience. Second, with older adults care should be taken in using large print for materials, allowing sufficient time for accomplishing tasks and course work, speaking slowly and face-to-face with adults, and making sure that the classroom has proper acoustics. Third, it is important to be well organized, to present material in a straightforward manner, and to avoid wasting time. Most adults are busy with a family, job, home, and friends. They expect that their continued education will be directed specifically to their learning needs.

SELECTED BIBLIOGRAPHY

Baird, H. W., Belt, D., Holder, L., & Webb, C. *A behavioral approach to teaching.* Dubuque, Iowa: Wm. C. Brown Co., 1970.

Charles, D. C. The older learner. *The Educational Forum,* 1971, *46* (2), 227-233.

Davis, L. N., & McCallon, E. *Planning, conducting and evaluating workshops.* Austin, Texas: Learning Concepts, 1974.

Dickinson, G. *Teaching adults: A handbook for instructors.* Toronto: New Press, 1973.

Ennis, R. H. *Logic in teaching.* Englewood Cliffs, New Jersey: Prentice-Hall, 1969.

Haddan, E. E. *Evolving instruction.* New York: Macmillan Co., 1970.

Johnson, S. R., & Johnson, R. B. *Developing individualized instructional material.* Palo Alto: Westinghouse Learning Press, 1970.

Kenneke, L. J., Nystrom, D. C., & Stadt, R. W. *Planning and organizing career curricula: Articulated education.* New York: Howard W. Sams & Co., 1973.

Miller, H., & Beasley, J. Seven ways to get a discussion going. *Teacher,* 1973, *91* (3), 35.

Miller, H., & Huck, J. *Delivering vocational instruction to adult learners.* Research project, Illinois State Office of Education, Division of Adult Vocational and Technical Education, and Southern Illinois University at Carbondale, College of Education, 1976.

Mississippi Council on Aging. *The aging process: An instructional handbook for teaching.* Jackson, Mississippi: Author, 1976.

National Association for Public Continuing and Adult Education. *A treasury of techniques for teaching adults.* Washington, D.C.: Author, 1964.

National Association for Public Continuing and Adult Education. *The second treasury of techniques for teaching adults.* Washington, D.C.: Author, 1970.

National Association for Public Continuing and Adult Education. *You can be a successful teacher of adults.* Washington, D.C.: Author, 1974.

Taba, H. *Curriculum development: Theory and practice.* New York: Harcourt, Brace & World, 1962.

8

Methods
for Adult Instruction

A variety of teaching methods can be used in adult classes. Some of the more important methods—explanations, demonstrations, questioning, drill, and tutoring—are examined in this chapter. The use of audiovisual methods has been omitted because a number of excellent guides are available (Brown, Lewis, & Harcleroad, 1977; Campeau, 1974; Kemp, 1975). No one method will suffice; all are needed, and frequently several should be used together in the same learning period. The goals to be achieved, the content to be taught, the characteristics of the chosen methods, and the learning capabilities of the adult students should determine the teaching technique. Adult learning will be as good as the methodology is effective in achieving objectives. In a real sense, the instruction determines the content because it is the means by which the content is delivered to the adult classroom.

EXPLANATION TECHNIQUES

One of the most criticized teaching techniques is the lecture method. Generally speaking, in the formal lecture, prepared material is presented to a class. Lectures provide the major part of course content, and students are expected to master this material. When used as the sole or major teaching technique, the lecture is generally ineffective compared to other methods. Its reliance on audio rather than visual communication, passive rather than participatory student role, group rather than individualized learning, and oral presentation rather than written and graphic information reduces the effectiveness of this method of teaching.

This does not mean that teacher talk needs to be avoided in the classroom; in fact, every adult teacher needs to become proficient in the explanation technique. Explanation is defined as description, interpretation, analysis, direction giving, and clarification in an informal and conversational manner.

The following functions are served by the explanation technique.

1. *Explanation emphasizes and reinforces information previously read and reviewed*—Explanations can be used as a means to aid adults in identifying and highlighting information that has already been presented or assigned. In Adult Basic Education or English as a Second Language, the adult instructor may wish to emphasize key comprehension rules already presented. In a carpentry class, the teacher can reinforce the procedure for hanging a door by outlining the key steps.

2. *Explanation synthesizes, abbreviates, and summarizes information presented*—When confronted with a mass of information encompassing examples, definitions, and exceptions, the adult teacher may want to synthesize and present the material that is most important to the class. This is especially desirable when adults are attempting to follow written directions. In a welding class, adults may have most of the skills needed in drawing a bead on two pipes. The teacher may find it necessary, however, to synthesize the directions from the book and emphasize the necessary skills needed for this particular welding task. At the end of a grocery-shopping unit in a consumer education course, the teacher may

state briefly the five basic rules that should be followed in weekly meal planning.

3. *Explanation adds information from other sources not readily available to the class*—Teachers may find that they need to bring to class additional information from several other sources. Because most ABE and GED courses use several different types of printed materials, the instructor will need to draw from many sources to provide this content. While reviewing various unions and procedures for joining a union, the teacher may decide to give the adults a brief historical description of trade unions in the area. A teacher may decide to provide additional information when student access to the material is inconvenient, when materials are not available at appropriate reading levels, or when only a limited number of copies is available. The decision must be made as to whether the added content should be oral or presented in some other form.

4. *Explanation clarifies information or specific points that are unclear or vague*—Explanation is a good teaching technique for assisting adults in understanding difficult material. Teachers may use explanation to reteach concepts and skills that are not understood. The procedure for converting fractions to percentages in a GED class, for example, frequently has to be discussed several times with the group to clarify the misunderstood areas of the process.

5. *Explanation repeats information already presented*—In adult education, many courses are brief. Although instructors do not want to make a common practice of conducting class sessions that duplicate information already learned, they may need to repeat information on occasion to reinforce the importance of the material. Reviewing for tests, reexamining basic information and skills, and assessing adults' progress within a unit are all reasons for repeating information.

6. *Explanation adapts previously learned information to new situations or to other content areas*—Explanations can point out exceptions and ramifications of material being studied. Especially with concepts and skills, time may be needed to relate new information to what has been previously studied by the class. Most mathematics skills can be adapted to consumer economics, for example.

What should be considered in planning the presentation? One of the first decisions involves what the adults are to achieve.

Without some means of determining what should be learned, the teaching will be aimless. In the explanation, it is important that the adults understand what is going to be presented and how this is related to what the class is studying.

Second, the teacher should use a brief outline that encompasses the points to be made. The presentation should not involve reading notes or memorizing content. Since people do not always speak in complete sentences, the adult teacher should not attempt to speak in unnatural, formal sentences. Conversational language and concise statements are a must. With regard to the style of speaking, the teacher can emphasize major points by being enthusiastic, using pauses, writing key words or phrases on the chalkboard or overhead projector, and providing an outline of major points. Moving around the room and maintaining eye contact are also very helpful. Learning is enhanced if the adults are encouraged to ask questions freely throughout the presentation.

Third, it is good to keep the presentations short—fifteen to twenty minutes at the most. If long explanations are necessary, the presentation should be broken up with practice sessions for the class. For a clear and precise presentation, material can be organized in terms of steps, manipulations, and behaviors. Undoubtedly, the more specific the adult teacher is, the more likely it is that adults will understand what is said and will be able to pinpoint what they do not understand. The presentation should be ended with a brief summary in the form of examples or a self-test.

DEMONSTRATIONS

Demonstrations show adults how something works and the procedure followed in using it. Demonstrations can supplement content, translate descriptive material into actual practice, and precede laboratory exercises.

The following are the primary functions of the demonstration technique.

1. *Demonstrations focus adult attention on correct procedure and application*—In many situations it is important—and sometimes imperative—that correct and accurate information and skills are learned. The demonstration is used as a means of illustration so that modeling and practice can take place. Because many adults, especially in ABE classes, have reading and comprehension problems in understanding directions, the demonstration is an essential teaching tool for conducting and implementing a procedure, skill, or method. Although methods of welding are described, the demonstration of the welding methods can facilitate understanding as well as allow for more accurate modeling of the methods. Nonverbally oriented adults can begin vocational and skill courses when course content is demonstrated for modeling practices.

2. *Demonstrations provide for an economical use of time, materials, and equipment*—Although it would be desirable to have a one-to-one teaching situation, it is often impossible to have a class consisting of a small number of adults. Also, the expense of some materials, equipment, and supplies calls for wise and economical use. Demonstrations provide a means to illustrate and clarify an approach, skill, and method to many adults at one time, without having all of the adults attempt the procedure. This may be the case, for example, with the use of stenographic equipment in office skills courses. The necessary equipment may not be available because few adults are interested in such a program or because a limited budget has precluded adding the equipment. A kiln for ceramics is an expensive investment for a self-enrichment program; therefore, ceramics courses may have a simulated demonstration of the glazing process. In addition, demonstrations can be effectively used to show a procedure as it would happen over a long period of time. The process can be speeded up to show the entire procedure, as in the case of varnishing.

3. *Demonstrations prepare adults for laboratory work and drill exercises*—Both laboratory work and drill exercises provide practice for skill improvement. Students watch the instructor perform the specific skill and then practice the skill themselves. Assessing and repairing brake problems, laying concrete for a patio, doing a watercolor picture, practicing English verb endings, and stating multiplication tables can all be demonstrated by the teacher before students practice in a laboratory setting.

4. *Demonstrations are a safe approach to teaching hazardous tasks*—Cracking acetylene and oxygen cylinders can be dangerous if not done properly. Wiring a home for a water heater also must be done cautiously and correctly. The demonstration is a way for the class to observe correct procedures and safety precautions which need to be taken. For extremely dangerous operations, adults may need to review the procedures several times before performing the skill. Demonstrations are also appropriate when working with precious metals or expensive materials. Cutting expensive stones, restoring paintings, and molding brass and gold are examples of operations demanding safety and care.

A key ingredient in the preparation of a demonstration is determining the precise steps which need to be observed. The demonstration should be visible, materials need to be available and ready, and the description should be presented in a clear and informal manner. If the adults are expected to repeat the demonstration immediately, enough equipment should be available. The number who will practice the demonstration should be small enough for proper supervision. The amount of work space and the amount of time needed by adults to do the assignment also must be taken into consideration. If adults are not able to perform the technique demonstrated, the teacher must find out what needs to be improved and repeated.

QUESTIONING TECHNIQUES

Questioning, whether oral or written, is one of the basic classroom teaching techniques available to adult teachers. Most adult teachers utilize this as a part of an approach to classroom instruction. Incorporated into the presentation method, the use of questions provides adult students and teachers an opportunity for exchanging and sharing information and ideas. The degree of adult participation in a course varies from answering an occasional question provides adult students and teachers an opportunity for several important functions.

1. *The use of questions can encourage exchanging and sharing adult views*—Through the exchange of differing views, tolerance, understanding, and appreciation can be developed. This may be especially important when attempting to support such value commitments as reporting to work on time, spending salary on necessities first, and passing the GED examination.

2. *Questioning enables the teacher to assess what adults already know, as well as what they need to learn*—The adult teacher can structure questions that reveal what adults know or do not know. Multiplication tables, vocabulary strength, and reading comprehension are a few content areas that are typically used with this type of questioning.

3. *Asking questions provides a way to explore and arouse adult interest and curiosity*—From questions and answers, the teacher can detect the degree of interest in the topic being studied. Questioning, furthermore, can be used to encourage adult interest by posing viewpoints unexplored by the class. Civil rights and personal freedoms are frequently high interest topics among adults studying the United States Constitution.

4. *The use of questions can serve to emphasize and reinforce the significant points of the information to be learned*—In many instances the teacher can use questions in a review session as a means of preparing a class for a test. Questioning in this form is quick and can be adjusted to a particular topic and to a particular class of students.

5. *Asking questions can be used to teach critical thinking*—By having adults consider implications or consequences of an action, the teacher encourages adults to organize their thoughts, to expand their ideas from the information presented, to speculate on what might be possible, and to form judgments.

6. *The use of questions calls for participation by adults*—By being asked to respond and contribute, adults are assuming an active role in the class. The frequent complaint by adult teachers that initiating class discussion is like pulling teeth may be the result of the quality and type of questions asked. Question asking may be looked at from two points of view: (1) the adult's position as the receiver of the question—did the adult understand what was asked, and (2) the teacher's position as the questioner—did the teacher construct the question in such a way as to communicate what was desired.

The Adult As Receiver of the Questions

An adult's response to a question will be determined by the context within which a question is asked, the knowledge possessed by the adults in the class when the question is asked, and the way the question is constructed. Frequently, it is assumed that a "why" question automatically causes thought and analysis. This is not always the case. If the answer to a "why" question is one that is previously known, thought and analysis will not take place. If, on the other hand, the class is unaware of the answer and is forced to use its own reasoning and skills, the question calls for a much different type of mental activity. The adult's awareness, capabilities, and existing knowledge, therefore, are important factors in drafting questions.

An adult's response will be determined to a large extent by how well the question is adapted to the adult's general ability. Several factors help determine whether a question is geared to a person's abilities.

1. *Vocabulary*—A good question uses words that are clearly understood by adults. Words that are academic and flowery and are not a part of the class's vocabulary only hinder the opportunity for class discussion. For the most part, it is best to approach question asking with ordinary, conversational language. By using a conversational approach, the teacher asks questions that not only are more easily understood, but also convey a genuineness in expression that will aid in developing a positive adult-instructor rapport. In gearing questions to adults' capabilities, a good teaching axiom is: "It is more important to have the class understand what is being asked than to avoid being asked."

2. *Wordiness*—A good question is succinctly stated and easily understood. The problem of losing adults in the middle of a question can be avoided by asking: "What is it that I am really trying to ask my class?" If key questions are well thought-out and prepared, wordiness and formality can be avoided in the teaching style.

3. *Adult interest*—Good questions are geared to the interest and maturity level of the class. To formulate more stimulating questions, a teacher will include such high-interest topics as: television, radio, sports,

cars, the family, welfare, and jobs.

4. *Leading questions*—Questions which indicate how the class should respond need to be avoided. Such questions as "Why did the Articles of Confederation fail?" and "Why can it be said that the United Nations is a failure?" indicate to the class that the teacher is seeking justification for a conclusion already drawn. A leading question, in effect, attempts to control and direct the discussion. A good questioner will assist adults in gaining insight, examining relationships, and developing their own conclusions.

The Adult Teacher As Initiator of Questions

Regarding the purpose and the type of question to be asked, several classification schemes have been designed for the adult teacher's use. The most noted scheme for question asking, Bloom's taxonomy of cognitive objectives, identifies six different levels of questions: (1) knowledge, (2) comprehension, (3) application, (4) analysis, (5) synthesis, and (6) evaluation. Although much research has been done to identify and distinguish among various types of questions, a basic criterion for good question asking rests on practicality and results. For this reason three types or levels of question asking are proposed—recall, evaluative, and creative. Each type calls for a different kind of mental activity by the class, and each requires different skills on the teacher's part.

Recall questioning. Recall questioning is the most frequently used technique and the easiest to formulate. Recall questions ask adults to retain, recognize, and memorize information. Questions of this nature have the advantage of aiding the instructor in determining the extent to which adults have mastered the subject matter. In subject areas like mathematics, foreign languages, and science, as well as many areas of the GED curriculum, recall questions give the teacher the opportunity to assess the class's level of understanding and readiness for new material.

Recall questions may be used to reinforce the material already learned. If the material is important, then reinforcement, practice, and repeated use can be a means for increasing retention. Learning the alphabet, as every teacher of English as a Second Language realizes, takes drill and practice. There is no magical formula for memorizing the ABCs.

The following verbs are used in recall questions: *state, name, identify, list, describe, relate, tell, recall, give,* and *locate.* In this type of questioning the adult generally is asked to provide a factual answer that can be easily checked as right or wrong. The following are examples of recall questions:

1. State in your own words what an additive inverse of a number is.
2. List three ways to join a corner in building a wood frame.
3. In what year was the Monroe Doctrine signed?
4. What can be used to check the charger unit for cordless appliances?

Questions beginning with *what, where,* and *how* are also recall questions. The demand on the student is to relate a previously learned place, happening, date, or cause.

Evaluative questioning. Evaluative questions ask adults to analyze information in accordance with some criteria in order to make a judgment. In such an activity, the teacher may either provide the criteria or have the class itself develop the criteria with which to make judgments. In either instance, the criteria would provide a means for adults to evaluate the worth and importance of the task at hand. The instructor attempts to promote systematic student examination and analysis of the issue or problem being studied. The advantages of using evaluation questions are: (1) they foster critical thinking and decision-making skills, (2) they promote adult interaction and discussion, and (3) they encourage adults to be concerned with personal and group values.

When asking evaluative questions, certain words help to identify and call for an evaluative answer. These words include: *evaluate, analyze, judge, compare/contrast, differentiate, calculate, measure, appraise, deliberate,* and *estimate.* Listed below are several examples of evaluation questions:

1. Evaluate the practice of dumping concrete into separate

piles within the form.
2. Differentiate between these two electrical symbols...
3. Compare the price for the best buy: two 12-oz. cans of tomato paste for $1.10 plus tax, and four 8-oz. cans of tomato paste for $2.00 plus tax.

Creative questioning. A third level of question asking involves having adults create or invent something different—something unique, new, and original to the adult. The purpose for using this level of activity is to urge adults to think beyond the subject matter being studied, to foster imagination, and finally to encourage adults to reach out beyond their experiences. The classroom which encourages creativity will exhibit the free interchange of ideas and support for a variety of views. Creative questioning uses the following words: *make, create, speculate, design, invent, construct, devise, predict, develop,* and *what would have happened if.* Examples of creative questions are:

1. What would have happened if the United States had not become involved in World War II?
2. Develop a different ending for this story.
3. Many geologists accept the continental drift theory; what other theories could explain the variety and distribution of plants?
4. Speculate on the reasons why the North American Indians didn't develop a technical society like that found in Europe.
5. Make a scale to determine the weight and volume of this object.

Creative question asking requires adults to use the information they possess to solve a particular problem. This solution should be original—at least for the student.

DRILL

Drill is a method of developing mastery through the repetitive learning of fixed answers to specific situations and conditions. Drill utilizes meaningful practice exercises to assist adults in learning new skills, enriching already acquired skills, and refining existing skills that are in need of redevelopment. The primary purpose of drill exercises, therefore, is to extend, reinforce, and refine an adult's capabilities to do specific mental and/or physical performances. By providing achievement feedback and by regulating the amount and number of practice sessions, the use of drill fosters higher levels of correct performance until mastery is complete.

The functions of drill include the following:

1. *Drill is a means for learning specific, demonstrable skills*—These performances (which may be listed and described in sequence or at random) are charactrized by processes, principles, rules, laws, designs, approaches, and methods. The ability to draw graphs, pronounce words, use rules of grammar, and apply mathematical computations are just a few examples of skills where performance would improve through drill exercises.

2. *Drill is a means for achieving mastery, proficiency, and improvement*—Mastery, proficiency, and improvement brought about by drill usually involve studied effort, rather than any innate learning capabilities of an exceptional nature. An adult with only normal physical and mental capabilities can increase the accuracy, precision, rate, and amount of learning to the desired level of proficiency. While it is recognized that such factors as age, motivation, fatigue threshold, and readiness influence the success of using drill in a given setting, the end result of continued use of drill is mastery. Typing, shorthand, drafting, filing, multiplication tables, and reading are examples of content in which mastery and proficiency can be brought about by drill.

Four different levels of drill exercises may be used for learning—model, recognition, construction, and transfer. Each level requires a greater degree of sophistication in skill answers than the preceding level. With each succeeding level, practice is provided that allows for expanded discretionary skill expression in terms of the type and quality of response.

Model exercises. Model drill exercises require adults to repeat accurately what has been presented to them. Copying, pronouncing, reproducing, and spelling are all examples of this type of drill activity. Model exercises insure accuracy of performance at a desired level and allow the instructor to present an exact reproduction of what is to be learned, followed by immediate student response. Foreign languages, vocabulary lists, mathematical processes and operations, music lessons and band rehearsals, physical education exercises, and penmanship exercises are instances that permit duplication and modeling procedures to be used adequately. Model exercises are generally used when introducing new subject matter. If the class takes the content in a piece-by-piece fashion, learning becomes more manageable. After the use of various demonstrations and mastery through drill, the increments of information can be integrated into a whole skill.

Recognition exercises. While modeling exercises are appropriate for introducing subject matter, recognition activities are geared primarily for reinforcing what has previously been learned. These exercises require an adult to demonstrate competence by differentiating between the desired material and that which is deemed unimportant or false. This level of drill requires the class to identify, note, select, and match those characteristics associated with the correct answer. Examples of recognition exercises include the selection of words that indicate a particular gender in a foreign language and matching the correct events of a particular historical period.

In writing recognition exercises, the formatting of incorrect answers is as important as constructing the correct answer. When an adult is to select the correctly spelled term from a series of similar terms, the teacher can construct an incorrect answer by spelling the term backward or by changing a component of the correct answer so that the option appears correct to the non-discriminating adult. A nonsense answer may be constructed with the components arranged in a nonsense order. Another approach is to provide an answer in which one or more components are omitted so that the reader needs to examine and respond on the basis of a supposed facsimile. A final approach for incorrect answers is to reverse two or more of the answer components. Such an approach is extremely useful when sequencing and ordering are important in performance proficiency.

Construction exercises.   Construction exercises generally are open-ended and demand that the class practice the correct answers with few, if any, clues to the correct response. In effect, adults have to organize, memorize, and respond with the performance or information requested with little assistance. When asked to list, demonstrate, and enumerate skill information, students are given few directions by the teacher. In some instances, the sequence of the answers given may be very important, while in other instances, it may be immaterial. Examples of this type of drill exercise include listing possible solutions for a specific situation, providing the verb tense for a verb in a foreign language, or performing certain gymnastic feats.

Construction exercises may fulfill many purposes. For one, such exercises require adults to perform a total skill with few cues. Adult students practice chaining specific responses and sequencing them into a framework based on minimal guidance from the teacher. The construction exercise may also be used to emphasize those previously learned skills that are not being applied by the adult in a comprehensive performance. Construction exercises can illustrate the importance of the various skill components. For example, in developing the arm motion for the sidestroke, the beginning swimmer can better understand the need for practicing separate arm movements when asked to demonstrate the sidestroke.

Transfer exercises.   Transfer exercises are designed to help adults apply and adapt acquired content and skills to a unique situation. Such exercises generally involve arrangement, measurement, assessment, analysis, construction, and decoration. Simulated as well as real-life assignments can be used in designing such exercises. When given transfer assignments, adults typically need to evaluate the situation, determine the needed content and skills, decide on an approach, and implement what has been learned.

Transfer exercises provide the class with practice in using what they have learned. This type of exercise may demand either specific replication or adaptation of skills. If a correct and incorrect transfer answer can be determined for a situation, specific replication is more likely to be necessary. When a situation is new and unique, adaptation and alteration of skills generally are involved in providing an appropriate answer.

Transfer exercises can take a variety of forms and can be used in most content areas. Instances of the appropriate use of transfer exercises include framing a house, interpreting and organizing information, tuning a car engine, drafting a plan for installing a heating system, evaluating art work, assessing a city's public transportation needs, and analyzing a school's curriculum. In each instance, the accomplishment of the task, the use of knowledge and skills, the level of performance, and the degree of adaptation can be determined and measured.

TUTORING

Tutoring is the individual instruction of one or more adults on an informal or formal basis. Such an instructional approach has been practiced by teachers, paraprofessionals, community volunteers, teacher aides, other members of the class, retired teachers, and college students. Tutoring can be provided in one subject or several. Tutoring can be used as a remedial technique to provide more directed learning, as a supplemental technique for interested class members, as an enrichment program for adults who desire to progress at a faster learning pace, and as a means for directing behavioral readjustments.

The tutoring process includes independent assignments and the assessment of those assignments, as well as teaching on a one-to-one basis. Both are considered tutoring since individualization is being provided. The functions of the tutoring process are as follows:

1. *Tutoring adjusts the method of teaching to the needs of the student*—Tutoring is individualizing teaching for the purpose of using the unique learning capabilities of members in the class. For visually-oriented adults who are learning how to read, tutoring through the use of word-picture cards is an appropriate technique.

2. *Tutoring encourages and motivates the individual*—Motivation is often difficult to achieve for ABE and GED adults. Embarrassment, resentment, a mistrust of institutional education, and the influence of friends and family are all strong factors in discouraging some adults from pursuing adult elementary and secondary education. Empathy, initiative, enthusiasm, and direction can be supplied by the tutor.

3. *Tutoring provides adults with immediate corrective feedback*—A major learning need for adults is to know if they have mastered the material. The instructor also needs to know if they have learned the material adequately before proceeding to the next unit. For most people, learning is not a one-time experience; they need to go over the material several times before they have mastered it. Feedback as to what has been learned and what needs to be taught again is crucial for most learning. In teaching a weaving course, it is important to know if the class can set up the looms before teaching the various weaving techniques. In a computer file management course, the instructor must be sure that each class member can use the codes for completing the information request forms. Vocabulary drill, conversations in a new language, and craft skills can be taught through the use of tutoring.

4. *Tutoring provides an atmosphere and a technique for involving adults in choosing, planning, and executing their learning activities*—An advantage of tutoring is that it does not necessarily require a large class-room but can be easily conducted in a variety of environments, large or small, formal or informal. Because the classroom can be perceived as a place of failure and resentment, tutoring can remove learning from the classroom setting. A further advantage is that tutoring can be used for involving adults in the learning process and providing for individual interests and specialized skill areas. The use of a newspaper for tutoring in reading improvement is an example of how individual reading interests may be accommodated.

How does one tutor? Not everyone can tutor, just as not everyone can teach. Tutoring needs to be structured to the individual capabilities of the adult. Tutors need to establish rapport on a one-to-one basis. They need to assess when adults should repeat, advance, or skip content. They need to structure and sequence learning experiences. Ability to change the environment, to use and prepare a wide variety of materials, and to emphasize basic learning skills are all important qualities for tutors. A good adage to follow in tutoring is that adults need to learn how to learn before they can use these skills to learn.

Effective tutoring requires content knowledge and an organized approach for translating the content to individual adults and their learning capabilities. Specifying instructional objectives, assessment of objectives, selection of content, use of drill exercises, and evaluating what has been learned are generally recognized as the necessary steps in the tutoring process. Accurate record keeping and a consistent tutoring schedule are also important for the adult teacher. For most tutorial instruction, records or diagnostic cards should be kept for each session indicating the objective being worked on, the amount of time devoted to the objective, and a progress statement. When content has been mastered, the date needs to be noted. Content that has been previously mastered needs to be reviewed periodically during the sessions.

Some adult teachers have developed their own standardized recording system which is used for all adults in a tutorial program. One such form is provided. Such forms need to be adapted to the content being taught and the type of recording desired.

Tutoring is an individualized approach to learning that focuses on verbal questions, explanations, and responses. The adult determines how much and how quickly he will progress. Tutoring is generally used in those teaching situations where the adult needs special assistance in learning. Although most adults can be taught by a tutoring technique, it is most effective in terms of class time when used to master difficult content.

NAME _____

TUTOR _____

SAMPLE ACHIEVEMENT PROFILE FOR MATHEMATICS

TOPICS	Computation Skills		Addition		Subtraction		Division		Multiplication		Fractions		Decimals		Measurement	
	Pre	Post	Pre	Post	Pre	Post	Pre	Post	Pre	Post	Pre	Post	Pre	Post	Pre	Post
DATE																
SCORE																
DATE																
SCORE																
DATE																
SCORE																
DATE																
SCORE																

Figure 8.1—Student Achievement Record

INQUIRY

Inquiry is a process by which the adult teacher and the adult student can evaluate information in order to arrive at some conclusion concerning important issues. It provides those skills by which reasoning can be directed towards ideas and may be thought of as problem solving. Typically, inquiry serves the following functions:

1. *Inquiry offers adults a way to seek information and make decisions in coping with social and personal problems*—Today's society is more than ever a rapidly changing one in which the adult citizen is confronted with numerous issues of monumental scope—racial conflicts, crime and delinquency, family disorganization, the growing centralization of government, and world social problems.

2. *Inquiry offers adult students a logical method of choice among the divergent interests, attitudes, and aspirations that surround them*—A pluralistic society offers alternatives from which adults must choose. Today's adult is faced with complex decisions characterized by a variety of options. There are few clear-cut issues.

3. *Inquiry provides needed skills for continuous life-long learning and problem solving*—The scientific and technical world of today has produced a society in which there is no longer a common body of information that can be transmitted.

4. *Inquiry encourages the development of creativity and freedom in the use of intelligence*—Traditional education, which emphasizes correct answers and memorization, has often restricted the use of human intelligence by stifling creativity and uniqueness in learning.

The opportunities for the use of inquiry occur in every adult classroom. In some instances inquiry can be initiated by the teacher, or it can be developed through the questions that adults raise in the class. Inquiry learning is composed of identifying a problem, formulating tentative solutions, organizing and evaluating information, and drawing conclusions from information.

Inquiry-oriented problems generally have one or more of the following characteristics:

1. *Persistent issue*—It has been, still is, and will be an important problem to a large number of people. The issue cannot be easily resolved.

2. *Controversial issue*—There may be conflicting interests, beliefs, and opinions surrounding the issue.

3. *Legitimate difference of opinion*—There are different attitudes and suggested courses of action.

4. *Need for complex thinking*—The problem requires the adult to perform at various levels, such as comparing, observing, classifying, interpreting, and looking for asumptions, as well as learning facts.

The first step in teaching an inquiry approach is to have adults identify and define a problem of interest and concern. Such a problem could be: "What should society do to insure the continuing availability of good usable water?" It is important that adults become involved in the problem situation. This can be done in a number of ways. The teacher may organize a discussion on why usable water is important. Presentations could be given on public and private solutions to a water pollution problem. The problem could be dramatized by relating it to the personal life of the adult, by presenting opposing points of view, by presenting data which appeal to adult interests, and by offering possible outcomes.

The second step in using inquiry is to formulate tentative solutions. The class should be encouraged to explain the problem in order to clarify it and to suggest necessary investigations to identify alternative solutions. The class should propose a statement as a possible solution. (The statement may be only a hunch, a guess, or an idea.) Hopefully, as the class becomes resourceful in suggesting possible solutions to the problem, they will become more self-reliant and more independent in their approach to decision making. Instead of depending on others for directions and decisions, adults will use the inquiry technique for their individual pursuits.

The third step in using inquiry is that the class gather information that is directed toward the solutions proposed. The class needs to organize and evaluate this information so that it either supports the proposed solutions or suggests other possible solutions. Possible ways to organize information include identifying relevant and irrelevant facts; identifying main and subordinate points; arranging ideas in some order, such as chronological, topical, or logical; and identifying relationships among a collection of facts. Recognizing cause-and-effect relationships, judging the validity and reliability of resources, supporting information from other evidence, and drawing parallels with historical facts are all ways to evaluate information.

The last step for the class is to draw conclusions from the information collected. If the solution originally proposed is substantiated by the information, it is accepted. When the solution is not substantiated by the information, the class needs to state a new solution to the problem suggested by the evidence and test it. Some questions that adults need to ask are:

1. Can the validity of the conclusions be substantiated by the evidence?
2. If the evidence indicates that the solution should be rejected, is a new solution available?
3. Will the conclusion reached be accepted as only tentative?
4. Are the contributions to the formation of conclusions considered legitimate and important?

Inquiry is a method of teaching which allows adult students to involve themselves actively in teaching and learning in the classroom. Inquiry is an excellent means for learning to examine social problems and attempting to identify workable solutions. The interests of the class can be readily accommodated by this means of instruction.

SMALL GROUPS

Adult instruction may take place in a variety of group settings, aside from typical classroom or tutoring sessions. The type of group setting used depends on the behavioral objectives, the degree of desired learning proficiency, the amount of instructional time needed, and the capability of adults to function in small groups.

   Brainstorming sessions encourage group members to generate a wide variety of ideas and possibilities. A good brainstorming session avoids criticism or evaluation of a particular idea. The intent of the session is to get the ideas placed before the group so that the merits of each idea can be considered at a later date. The adult teacher's responsibility in a brainstorming group is to motivate discussion and presentation of ideas. For the most part, the adult teacher remains out of the discussion and facilitates group process as necessary. A configuration of how a brainstorming group typically appears is shown in the following figure.

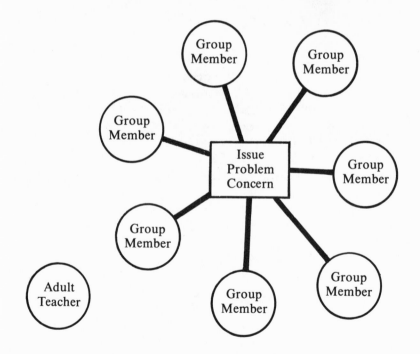

Figure 8.2—**Brainstorming Groups**

A second general type of small group is the discussion group. Unlike brainstorming sessions, the discussion group includes the adult teacher who interacts frequently with other group members. Typically, the adult teacher starts the discussion. In some instances, a brief introduction to the issue is given along with a few salient questions. Most discussion groups consider issues, problems, and concerns which involve values rather than factual answers. Typically, an answer is not obvious, and the group needs to search it out. As the members of the group assume more responsibility for the discussion, the adult teacher does more listening, refocusing the discussion only when necessary. The adult teacher clarifies, probes, and channels discussion topics. A typical discussion group configuration appears in the following manner.

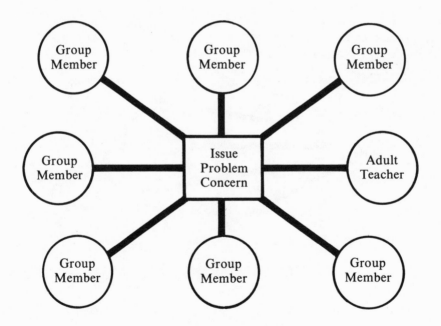

Figure 8.3—**Discussion Group**

A tutorial group is a third type of group organization. Instead of working with just one adult student, a tutor works with four or five adults needing or desiring special assistance. Generally, the more common and specific the learning need is among adults, the more likely the tutorial group can be used effectively. Further, when confronted with a large class and the need for tutorial sessions, this type of group organization can accommodate more adults. Paraprofessionals and volunteers can also be used for teaching in this type of setting. With tutorial grouping, factual recall and drill exercises are normally the learning focus. The following diagram illustrates a tutorial group configuration.

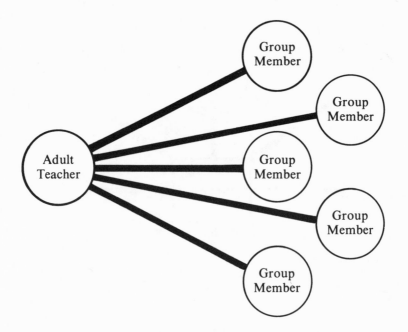

Figure 8.4—**Tutorial Group**

The number of group members may vary depending upon the total number of adults in the class, the objectives for the lesson, and the content to be taught. The group's composition may be altered to provide greater learning and to encourage peer teaching and self-help. Adults may be grouped according to random assignments or according to ability, sex, age, confidence, or knowledge. The number of participants and the type of instruction presented should be varied enough so that adults do not feel that they are being stereotyped according to learning ability. Grouping is a form of individualizing instruction, and it should be used for the benefit of the adult student.

SELECTED BIBLIOGRAPHY

Bergevin, P., Morris, D., & Smith, R. M. *Adult education procedures.* New York: Seabury Press, 1963.

Bloom, B. S., et al. *Taxonomy of educational objectives, the classification of educational goals, handbook I: Cognitive domain.* New York: David McKay, 1956.

Brown, J. W., & Lewis, R. B. *A V instructional technology manual for independent study* (5th ed.). New York: McGraw-Hill, 1977.

Brown, J. W., Lewis, R. B., & Harcleroad, F. F. *A V instruction: Technology, media, and methods* (Rev. ed.). New York: McGraw-Hill, 1977.

Burrichter, A. W., & Ulmer, C. (Eds.). *Special techniques that work in teaching the culturally deprived.* Englewood Cliffs, New Jersey: Prentice-Hall, 1972.

Campeau, P. L. Selective review of the results of research on the use of audiovisual media to teach adults. *A V Communication Review,* 1974, *22* (1), 5-40.

Cass, A. W. *Basic education for adults.* New York: Association Press, 1967.

Cloward, R. D. Studies in tutoring. *The Journal of Experimental Education,* 1967, *36* (1), 14-25.

Deep, D. Individualized learning for adults: The ILA Project. *Adult Leadership,* 1972, *20* (8), 291.

Dewey, J. *Logic: The theory of inquiry.* New York: Holt, Rinehart & Winston, 1938.

Dickinson, G. *Teaching adults: A handbook for instructors.* Toronto: New Press, 1973.

Grabowski, S. M. Methods and techniques in adult education. *Adult Leadership,* 1970, *19* (3), 99-100.

Kaplan, A. *The conduct of inquiry: Methodology for behavioral science.* San Francisco: Chandler Publishing Co., 1964.

Kemp, J. *Planning and producing audiovisual materials* (3rd ed.). New York: Thomas Y. Crowell, 1975.

Klevins, C. (Ed.). *Materials and methods in adult education.* New York, Klevens Publications, 1972.

Knowles, M. *Modern practice of adult education.* New York: Association Press, 1970.

Lloyd, J. H. *A handbook for teachers of adults.* Washington, D.C.: Federal City College, 1972.

Miller, H., & Vinocur, S. How to ask classroom questions. *School and Community,* 1973, *59* (6), 10.

Miller, H. G., et al. *Drill re-examined: A taxonomy for drill exercises lab book.* Carbondale: Southern Illinois University, 1974. (ERIC Document Reproduction No. ED 103 311)

Miller, H. L. *Teaching and learning in adult education.* New York: Macmillan Co., 1964.

National Association for Public Continuing and Adult Education. *The second treasury of techniques for teaching adults.* Washington, D.C.: Author, 1970.

National Association for Public School Adult Education. *Adult Basic Education: A guide for teachers and teacher trainers.* Washington, D.C.: Author, 1967.

Smith, E. *Literacy education for adolescents and adults.* San Francisco: Boyd and Fraser, 1970.

Suchman, J. R. *Developing inquiry.* Chicago: Science Research Associates, 1966.

Ulmer, C. *Teaching the disadvantaged adult.* Washington, D.C.: National Association for Public School Adult Education, 1969.

Verduin, J. R., Jr. *Conceptual models in teacher education,* Chapter 11. Washington, D.C.: American Association of Colleges for Teacher Education, 1967.

Von Harrison, G. *Supervisor's guide for the structured tutorial reading program.* Provo, Utah: Brigham Young University Press, 1972.

Waite, N. ABE methods. In W. M. Brooke (Ed.), *Adult Basic Education.* Toronto: New Press, 1972.

9
Evaluation in Adult Instruction

―――――――――――――――――

E valuation is a fundamental aspect of adult instruction. Without evaluation the adult instructor has no information on the growth of students or the success of the instructional enterprise. This chapter focuses on how to evaluate adults and their learning and how to construct various measurement instruments to use in the process.

MEANINGS OF EVALUATION

Evaluation is the process of assessing an adult's progress and achievement of objectives. Generally, evaluation means the designing, writing, and administering of various instruments to assess the learning of knowledge, skills, and attitudes. Evaluation is necessary to determine the extent to which the desired changes in behavior have been achieved. It is the attempt to measure the behaviors specified in the objectives. Successful evaluation not only indicates achievement, but also reflects and provides information on the degree of instructional effectiveness.

Many functions are served by the use of evaluation. First and foremost, an evaluation provides data from which to make a judgment concerning the degree of demonstrable achievement. An in-progress evaluation occurs at frequent intervals during a period of instruction so that instruction may be altered if necessary. This evaluation process, termed formative, also provides information about the further learning needs of an adult. The teacher should provide adults with immediate feedback of test scores, since delaying performance results normally hinders learning.

The terminal evaluation process, referred to as summative evaluation, is done at the end of an instructional plan, unit, course, or program, Usually, with terminal evaluations, no further opportunity exists for instructional remediation. However, it does provide a means of improving future instruction and modifying future instructional plans. It also provides data on the behavior of the adult at the end of some instructional activity.

Information collected from an evaluation is also a basis for assessing the effectiveness of instruction. The purpose of instruction is to facilitate learning, and the purpose of evaluation is to determine the extent of learning. The quality of instruction is determined to a great extent by the results obtained from evaluations.

Evaluation may also be used in making decisions about the practicality of a course or program. It can document the need for the content being taught. If a preassessment indicates that adults already have the specific knowledge, skills, and attitudes desired, instruction is not necessary. In this sense evaluation is an indication of adult readiness for learning new things.

The results from evaluations may also be used for placement of adults with prospective employers, for diagnosing more advanced learning needs, and for vocational and career decision making. This information aids counselors in helping adults to make rational decisions regarding vocational aspirations and also aids employers in selecting personnel.

Finally, evaluation is a source for enhancing adult motivation.

Success generates a sense of achievement and develops an adult's confidence in learning. The desire for further and more advanced learning is reinforced. If evaluations indicate that an adult is not progressing as well as expected, remedial work can be assigned and instructional techniques revised so that an adult will not become discouraged with his lack of progress.

PROGRAM AND INSTITUTION EVALUATION—GENERAL LEVEL

The demand for fiscal and curricular accountability is fostering the need for more precise evaluations of adult programs, institutions, and systems. Evaluation at this educational level is often a self-evaluation process whereby staff members themselves determine the degree to which they are successful in implementing the overall intent of courses and instructional plans. The procedures described in this section are a means for making a self-evaluation.

When undertaking an evaluation of a program, institution, or system, the staff members begin by identifying the central objective of the institution or system. For the most part statements of purpose or objectives of adult education programs tend to be broad and all-encompassing. Frequently, statements of purpose emphasize providing training in such areas as civic responsibility, basic learning skills, self-sufficiency, critical thinking, and rehabilitation. Typical statements include:

The center shall endeavor to provide those learnings and activities which foster constructive membership in society.

The institution has a primary commitment to develop self-sufficiency and job skills of those clientele in attendance at the facility.

The program is for the enhancement of personal interests and skills and for self-enrichment and personal growth.

The meaning of an objective may be identified by reducing the statement to key words or phrases. Once the central idea has been noted, the next step is to identify information available within the total institution that can be used to measure the level of accomplishment of the objective. What tangible evidence is available which supports the objective? What types of information would be the most desirable as a demonstration of accomplishment? The following are examples of information which could be sought:

Results from standardized tests
Number of adults placed in jobs
Registration for self-enrichment courses
Participation of lay citizens in the center's activities
Referrals to the institution by other community agencies

The next step is to indicate the method of quantification. The intent of quantification is to provide a means for examining a particular type of information. Determining a criterion necessitates quantifying the information in terms of percentages, amount, duration, proportion, rates, sums, or scores. The evaluators need to determine how the numerical data should be examined and organized to present the most accurate picture possible of an institution's progress. Examples of specific types of information to be computed are:

Average scores on the GED test

Percentage of adults placed in jobs compared to the total number of adults completing the job skills program

Number of adults referred to the program from other community agencies; percentage of adults accepted into the adult education program

Number and percentage of adult students completing the GED test

With the types of information selected and the means of measurement determined, the next and final task is to identify the sources from which evidence may be obtained; that is, determining where, how, and from whom information is available. Sources may be individual teachers of adults, professional adult education organizations, adults who have graduated from programs, janitors in a building, and many others. In some instances, it might be necessary to identify just the location of the information, such as the director's office or the guidance office files. It should be realized that some desired information may not be available due to a lack of record keeping.

Systematically outlining what has been happening is not the same as determining the degree of success of an adult education program. An adult education institution and program may be evaluated in a number of ways. First, the information collected for one term or semester may be used as a baseline for comparing with information collected in succeeding terms. With greater occurrence from one term to the next, improvement and greater effectiveness may be argued. Second, a norm or standard of achievement can be set. By comparing actual performance with what is defined as the desired outcome, achievement can be assessed.

In summary, approaches to evaluating practices and philosophies of an adult education program include: (1) identifying the central purpose of the institution's philosophy and general goals, (2) identifying the types of information reflective of the institution and system, (3) identifying a means of measuring the types of information with criteria, and (4) identifying the sources from which information may be obtained.

EVALUATION FOR COURSES AND INSTRUCTIONAL PLANS—INTERMEDIATE AND SPECIFIC LEVELS

There are a variety of tests, test items, and test construction procedures for evaluating courses and instructional plans. Two general types of tests for assessing entering and terminal performance are common. One type is the standardized test. Standardized tests have uniformity in terms of item construction, test administration and scoring, and score interpretation through the use of test norms. These special features are achieved by sampling a large population over a period of time. These tests are especially useful in comparing results using such variables as age, education level, and sex; in assessing learning over a long period of time; and in diagnosing entering behavior capability and performance level. Standardized tests are generally available from publishing companies and testing services and include a variety of types: intelligence tests which render an IQ percentile rank, achievement tests which show a subject-area attainment level, interest inventories in various fields which reflect likes and dislikes, aptitude tests which measure potential for certain skill or occupational areas, and personality tests which measure personality traits. Many standardized tests require trained personnel to administer and to interpret the results. In some instances, tests are scored and interpreted by the publishing company.

Although many standardized tests are available for use, teacher-made tests are the most commonly used in adult education learning situations. For the most part, such tests are designed by individual teachers for their own teaching needs. Standardized tests have the advantage of professional test writers and a support service for test validation. Teacher-made tests can be adapted to specific behavioral objectives, given at frequent intervals, constructed and scored easily, and developed to assess the particular experiences of adults in a learning program. Further, teacher-made tests can be used as an indicator of instructional effectiveness. Since most of the testing done in adult education is with teacher-made tests, the remaining sections of this chapter are devoted to techniques for constructing test items for specific learning needs.

CONSTRUCTING OBJECTIVE TEST ITEMS

For objective test items the correct answer can be determined and will be the same for all adults when the content has been mastered. The advantages frequently associated with this type of item are that it can encompass a wide range of content, it identifies responses that are clearly correct or incorrect minimizing subjective scoring, and it can be scored easily with an answer key. This allows adults to have their test results within a short period of time. The limitations of using objective test items are: (1) they lead to guessing in some instances, (2) they may emphasize trivia, and (3) they limit the types of learning that can evaluated. Objective tests are frequently time-consuming to construct; but once they are written, they can be added to a test item list for future use and improvement. Objective test items can be validated in terms of behavioral objectives and can be measured for reliability to see if different groups over a period of time have similar test results.

Multiple-Choice

A multiple-choice item is an incomplete statement, a question, or symbols and mathematical problems followed by a listing of three to five responses. The adult selects the response that best completes the statement, answers the question, or solves the problem. Generally, the adult is asked to write the number or letter of the chosen response in the space provided.

Examples of multiple-choice test items are:

__(b)__   1.   Fish is

        a.   a form of vegetable
        b.   a form of protein
        c.   a form of poultry
        d.   a form of pork

__(d)__   2.   What does ABE mean?

        a.   Adults for Broader Education
        b.   Americans for Basic Education
        c.   Alternative Basic Education
        d.   Adult Basic Education

__(e)__   3.   Add 400,111; 376,271; 542,181; and 721,000.

        a.   1,039,563
        b.   2,339,563
        c.   3,339,563
        d.   2,009,563
        e.   None of the above

In constructing responses, teachers can write foils (i.e., incorrect responses) in a number of ways. A foil, for example, can be a nonsense response, a minor adaptation of the answer, a response that is an answer to another item, and a "none of the above" or "all of the above" response. A teacher needs to be careful when using the phrase "all of the above" as a response since all of the other responses need to unambiguously correct. The foils used are very important because they help validate the test item. If the foils do not discriminate between adults who know the answer and those who do not, the item is not serving its purpose.

In constructing multiple-choice items, four or five responses are preferable to minimize guessing and reflect content mastery. Correct answers should be placed at random so that response patterns can be avoided. Many multiple-choice tests, for example, have the correct answer in the middle of the responses, especially in the *b* and *c* range. The correct answer should be clearly provided among the foils. Content which is disputed and open for interpretation needs to be avoided unless the authority expressing the position is identified. Long, involved responses also need to be avoided. Responses need to have parallel grammatical structure.

Multiple-choice testing provides the following advantages: (1) it maximizes test item discrimination while minimizing the accuracy of guessing, (2) it provides convenient scoring by hand or by machine, and (3) it has an easy response format. These advantages make the multiple-choice format the most widely used type of test.

Matching

Matching test items involve the pairing of items in two groups usually in the form of lists or columns. Typically, the adult is asked to identify the relationship by placing the letter of the factor in one group next to the corresponding factor in another group. Instead of writing numbers or letters, some matching items ask adults to draw a connecting line between the paired factors. The most common form of matching uses columns as in these three examples.

Proofreaders' Marks

_____	1. Capitalize	a.	⊙
_____	2. Ragged margin	b.	ℙ
_____	3. Close up	c.	⊂
_____	4. Comma	d.	st. louis
_____	5. Begin paragraph	e.	❩
_____	6. Let it stand	f.	⌃
_____	7. Period	g.	stet

Electrical Symbols

_____	1. Lamp	a.	S_3
_____	2. Motor	b.	Ⓛ
_____	3. Light fixture	c.	—(M)—
_____	4. Ground	d.	⊖
_____	5. Wire connected	e.	≡
_____	6. Three-way switch	f.	—●—

Money Identification

_____1.	Ten-dollar bill	a.	Abraham Lincoln
_____2.	One-dollar bill	b.	Gerald Ford
_____3.	Twenty-dollar bill	c.	George Washington
_____4.	Five-dollar bill	d.	Ulysses S. Grant
_____5.	Fifty-dollar bill	e.	Franklin D. Roosevelt
		f.	Thomas Jefferson
		g.	Andrew Jackson
		h.	Theodore Roosevelt
		i.	Alexander Hamilton
		j.	Dwight D. Eisenhower

Matching items (terms or short phrases) may be written on the basis of dates-events, elements-properties, terms-definitions, author-writings, parts-functions, and foreign words-English counterparts. This type of test item also may use pictures, symbols, diagrams, and maps. Generally, both columns contain the same number of items, but in some instances more options may be provided to limit matching by the process of elimination.

Matching test items are especially useful when the content contains a large number of significant relationships and when these relationships are identified as a part of the behavioral objectives. Matching test items may be easily written and scored, take up little space on the paper, cover a broad range of factual content, require little writing on the part of the student, and are usually free from ambiguity.

True-False

True-false test items are sometimes referred to as alternative-response items in which two response options to a statement are possible for the adult taking a test. The responses may be true-false, right-wrong, or yes-no. The adult is to distinguish whether or not the item if factually accurate as written. Variety in marking a response is possible, as noted in the examples provided.

F   T   1.   The official abbreviation for Alabama is AL.
F   T   2.   Cheyenne is the capital of Wyoming.
___Right   3.   One of the activities of the Federal Trade
___Wrong   Commission is to prevent unfair business
                   competition and practices.
Yes No   4.   A notary public is an elected position.
Yes No   5.   *Van, de,* and *El* in foreign names are referred
                   to as the person's Christian name.

In writing true-false test items, the teacher should avoid words like *always, totally, never, absolutely, usually,* and *frequently.* A statement which uses the word *always,* for example, tends to be false since the word implies that no exceptions are permissible. Questions need to be straight-forward and reflect a significant point rather than dwell on trivia or involve trick statements.

Completion

Completion test items are statements in which major terms or phrases are omitted and replaced by a blank space. Given these statements, adults are asked to recall and write in the correct term or phrase. Completion test items can be in the form of a question or a sentence. Most items of this type require that the response be written either in the blank provided within the statement itself or alongside the statement in a column fashion which would facilitate scoring. Answers may be one or more words, but the blanks provided for all items should be the same length so that the amount of space is not perceived as a cue to the word(s) needed. Examples of this type of test item are:

1.   (White flour) is the food prepared by grinding and bolting cleaned wheat with removal of up to 28 percent of the branny layers.

2. The 35 national parks in the National Parks System, administered by the ___ (National Park Service) ___ of the United States Department of the Interior, generally require an entrance fee.
3. The appliance industry has established a mechanism for handling complaints about major appliances which is called (Major Appliance Consumer Action Panel) .
4. The (Home Ventilating Institute) , an organization whose membership consists of manufacturers of residential ventilation guidelines, has certified ratings of home ventilation equipment.

This type of test item has many advantages. For one, it reduces guessing by not providing responses for selection. It asks for reconstruction of the answer from memory rather than by means of comparison. For another, completion test items can be used with a variety of factual content, and they are easy to use especially with printed material. Writing completion test items is fairly easy and quick to do.

CONSTRUCTING ESSAY TEST ITEMS

An essay test item requires adults to compose a descriptive answer on a blank piece of paper using their own words. Generally, an essay question takes several written paragraphs to answer. Both the quality of writing and the answer itself are important in scoring.

The most common types of essay items are:

1. *Compare and contrast*—Asks adults to explain and describe similarities and differences between certain factors mentioned in the question
2. *Criticism*—Calls for a critical analysis of weaknesses, limitations, differences, and inadequacies
3. *Summary*—Requires adults to recall information previously learned, to identify elements of that information relevant to the question, and to report the information in abbreviated form.

4. *Recommendations*—Asks adults to analyze a problem, issue, or event and draft a solution or course of action based upon their analysis

Examples of essay test items are numerous.

1. Compare and contrast asphalt with wood shingles.
2. Critically review the 1976 edition of *Shopper's Guide*.
3. Write a summary of Bolt's position on interior decorating for the home.
4. Given a rectangular living room of 200 square feet with no windows, make some suggestions for decorating.

Essay test items are appropriate for measuring complex behavior since adults must explain in their own words relationships, data, or conclusions. Adults have more freedom to construct an answer that reflects their own ideas and writing style.

Writing essay items is generally thought to be easier than writing objective test items; however, it is more difficult than presumed. There are some rules that should be considered when constructing essay questions. The essay item should be written in a clear manner and state a definite task to the adult. The teacher should allow ample time for the student to organize and write the response. Adults vary in their ability to handle these functions; some will need more time than others. Instead of having adults write on two or three essay items, it may be preferable for them to write on only one item.

CONSTRUCTING PERFORMANCE TEST ITEMS

Adult teachers frequently need to use testing situations and test items which are not oriented to textbooks or printed material alone. Skill performance of a task and completion of a project are difficult to evaluate with paper-and-pencil tests. Methods for observing and evaluating student performance must be developed by the teacher of adults. While performance tests cannot be validated in the same manner as objective test items, measurement can be achieved by establishing and applying predetermined criteria. Such criteria could be selected and developed from the following:

1. The uniqueness (creativity) of the completed task
2. The amount of time taken to perform the task
3. The amount of effort expended in the task
4. The use of certain principles or concepts in the task
5. The amount of planning and preparation done for the task
6. The quality and effectiveness in communicating the completed task
7. The accuracy in the application of specific methods as represented in the task
8. The degree to which logical construction took place or is taking place in the task
9. The number of differing components employed in the task

Determining appropriate criteria for a performance test is an essential factor for evaluation. One approach to determining appropriate criteria is to list those indispensible features which would be needed to complete the given activity successfully. By answering the question, "As an adult teacher, what are my expectations for a well done task," the teacher can compile and describe the desirable characteristics needed. Once a task has been evaluated a number of times, the criteria can be modified or revised according to what adults can actually accomplish. The type of assignment given by the adult teacher may also aid in determining appropriate criteria. A task which asks adults to demonstrate the use of specific methods may emphasize an adult's competency rather than the effort involved in attaining that competency. If the assignment involves quality and amount of work (such as constructing a model), effort may be a crucial criterion of success.

Checklists

A checklist is one device that can assist the teacher in evaluating performance based on specific criteria. A checklist is an observational tool which allows for seeing and recording the presence and absence of behaviors, characteristics, or events in specific learning situations. Instruments of this nature generally rely on observing exhibited performance, call for "yes-no" or "present-absent" judgments, and can indicate whether or not a sequence of behaviors is achieved.

Activities included in a checklist should be clearly stated and should reflect the most important components of the task. The more clearly the actions are described, the more accurate the learning assessment can be. The use of action words in the description reduces misunderstanding and clarifies intentions. Behavioral objectives are an appropriate beginning point for compiling a checklist.

Here are two examples of checklists.

Checking A Car Engine's Oil Level

Name_____   Date_____

Observer _____

Did	Did Not		Activities
_____	_____	1.	Turn car engine off.
_____	_____	2.	Put car in park position.
_____	_____	3.	Open hood of car and remove dipstick.
_____	_____	4.	Wipe oil off dipstick.
_____	_____	5.	Reinsert dipstick in hole.
_____	_____	6.	Remove dipstick.
_____	_____	7.	Check the oil marking.
_____	_____	8.	If oil level is at "add oil" or above, the oil is OK.
_____	_____	9.	If oil level is below "add oil," oil should be added.

Making Pineapple Squares

Name_____ Date_____

Observer _____

✓ completed

_____ 1. Drain 1 cup crushed pineapple.
_____ 2. Mix 2½ cups graham cracker crumbs with ¼ pound of melted butter.
_____ 3. Spread crackers/melted butter in a 9" x 13" pan.
_____ 4. Bake in an oven for 10 minutes at 350°F.
_____ 5. Cool for fifteen minutes.
_____ 6. Mix 1½ cups of powdered sugar with ¼ pound of butter and 2 eggs.
_____ 7. Spread sugar, butter, and egg mixture over first layer.
_____ 8. Whip ½ pint of cream and add drained pineapple.
_____ 9. Spread cream and pineapple over second layer.
_____ 10. Viola!

A checklist should be convenient to use and mark. The best format is to have a space to check next to the action being observed. A check can be made when the action occurs, or a numbering system can be used to indicate the sequence in which the actions occurred. The amount of time taken for the action to occur is sometimes desirable to note, especially with time-oriented activities. Some checklists provide space for noting errors. It may be desirable to know not only what is done but also what is not done so that additional instruction can be provided. In evaluating a speech, for example, it might be important to check whether or not physical gestures are used to emphasize particular points.

Rating Scales

A rating scale, like a checklist, is an observational tool which uses a scale to indicate the quality or level of performance observed. The behaviors, characteristics, and actions are known in advance of the observation; and the observer's attention is focused on specific aspects or components. Examples of two rating scales are provided.

PART I.   PHILOSOPHY AND OBJECTIVES

a. Objectives are: (Lo)1   2   3   4   5(H)

...congruent with philosophy   ____ ____ ____ ____ ____

...consistent with available
resources   ____ ____ ____ ____ ____

...consistent with community
needs   ____ ____ ____ ____ ____

...consistent with adult needs   ____ ____ ____ ____ ____

...revised continuously   ____ ____ ____ ____ ____

...stated in form conducive
to measurement   ____ ____ ____ ____ ____

TENNIS EXECUTIONS

1. Hit a forehand drive

| Poor | Below Average | Average | Above Average | Excellent |

2. Hit a forehand lob

| Poor | Below Average | Average | Above Average | Excellent |

3. Hit a backhand drive

| Poor | Below Average | Average | Above Average | Excellent |

4. Hit a backhand lob

| Poor | Below Average | Average | Above Average | Excellent |

Different types of scales may be used as seen in the two examples. The most common scale is a numerical form. The teacher checks or circles a number to indicate degree or frequency. Usually, a number scale is given descriptors indicating value or at least a high-low direction, as shown in the following example.

1. To what extent was the jump done with precision?
    (Lo)1   2   3   4   5(H)

A second way to apply criteria is to delineate a scale in descriptive terms so that each criterion is clearly defined. The descriptions on the scale are usually stated as behavioral objectives. This is the most difficult form of rating scale to write; however, it has the best communication value. In this example, neatness is marked excellent when the completed task contains no typographical errors, a cover page, 1½-inch margins on both sides of the paper, and a manila folder. Although each adult teacher has to decide what constitutes neatness, adults have the benefit of knowing exactly what is expected of them in completing their tasks. A descriptive scale would appear as follows:

NEATNESS

Poor	Average	Excellent

Poor—Many corrected/uncorrected typographical errors, may have a cover page, margins are one inch or less, and a folder may or may not be used.

Average—Some corrected typographical errors, a cover page, over one-inch margins on both sides of the paper but not the margins suggested, and placed in a manila folder.

Excellent—No typographical errors, a cover page, 1½-inch margins on both sides of the page, and placed in a manila folder.

The adult teacher may want to weight the criteria if certain criteria are more important than others. For example, while effort may be considered a necessary criterion, the application of specific methods may be of greater importance. Given this type of situation, the application of specific methods could be given double value. Effort, in this instance, could be ranked one through five, whereas application could be rated one through ten. In this way, the adult teacher conveys that certain aspects of the assignment will be stressed more than others.

In using a rating scale, teachers should be aware of the tendency to be overly generous in rating, to compare one student's performance or product with others, or to avoid using the extreme positions on the rating scale. If this is felt to be a problem, it is helpful to have several people do independent ratings and to calculate an average. (A numerical scale may have to be substituted for descriptors in this case.) The average becomes the rating for the performance or product. This approach with modifications is frequently used in judging sports events.

Anecdotal Records

The anecdotal record is a brief account of some event that is happening or has happened. It is a factual description and might be thought of as a word picture of an incident. A good anecdotal record keeps the objective description of an incident separate from any interpretation of the meaning of the behavior.

Anecdotal records are an effective tool for observations of unanticipated actions or incidents in the skill performance area. They allow for collecting information of actual behavior in natural situations. The form provides space to identify the date, time, name of the observer, and what or whom is being observed. There should be a space for a description of the incident and also a space for indicating the setting in which the event occurred. Following is an example of an anecdotal form which might be of use.

Anecdotal Record Form

Name _____ Date _____

Observer _____ Time _____

Setting_____

Incident:

What supporting information is available?

Date _____

Time Finished _____

If a number of anecdotal observations or recordings are made of the same event, incident, or product, it is necessary to compile these recordings into one summary for making interpretatons and recommendations. A common summary form following that format is shown here.

Anecdotal Record Summary

Name _____

Observer(s) _____

_____

This summary is based on _____ records
                              (No. of records)

Is there supporting information on file? yes _____ no _____

If yes, where is information located?_____

_____

Summary statement:

Recommendations:

For anecdotal records to be useful, descriptions need to be accurate and clear. Observers need to be trained in this technique. The person making the observation should record the incident as soon after it occurs as possible. If each written anecdote is restricted to a brief single incident, the description tends to be more accurate. A number of anecdotes will need to be recorded before any inferences can be made.

DETERMINING ACHIEVEMENT LEVELS

Specifying performance and constructing evaluation tests are necessary but not sufficient to determine if learning has been achieved. The adult's performance must be compared with some standard. Selection of the standards to be employed in judging an adult's learning is a vital factor in the evaluation process.

Typically, two types of standards have been employed in determining the degree of adult learning. These two types of standards are referred to as norm-referenced and criterion-referenced. In *norm-referenced systems,* the adult's achievement is compared to the achievement of a group of adults. In a norm-referenced system an adult who learns 20 percent of the subject matter while others learn only 10 percent is performing above average even though he has mastered very little of the subject matter. On the other hand, if the majority of adults have learned 99 percent of the material and one adult has learned 90 percent, that person is performing below average despite a high mastery of the subject matter. In other words, norm-referenced systems assess individual performance in relation to the performance of others and not to the total amount of material learned. Norm-referenced standards rank adults in terms of group performance.

In a *criterion-referenced system,* the adult's performance is compared to absolute predetermined standards normally established by the adult teacher. If the adult teacher, for example, has established the criterion at 90 percent mastery of the material, the adult who achieves this level of mastery is said to have learned the material regardless of the number of other adults also meeting the criterion. Likewise, an adult who completes only 50 percent of the material correctly has not mastered the material despite the fact that he may have performed better than any other adult.

Two basic subcategories of criterion-referenced systems are presently in use. The first is labeled a "one-shot system": the standards are established, and the adult is given a single opportunity to achieve the standard that has been set. After completing the exercise, the adult is assigned an achievement level based upon his test score. In the "mastery system" the standards are established, and the adult is free to continue studying and to repeat examinations until he achieves mastery at the desired or minimally acceptable level of performance.

SELECTED BIBLIOGRAPHY

Anderson, S. B., Ball, S., Murphy, R. T., et al. *Encyclopedia of educational evaluation.* San Francisco: Jossey-Bass Publishers, 1975.

Bloom, B. S. Learning for mastery. *Evaluation Comment,* 1968, *1* (2), 1-12.

Bloom, B. S., Hastings, J. T., & Madaus, G. F. *Handbook on formative and summative evaluation of student learning.* New York: McGraw-Hill Book Co., 1971.

Buros, O. K. (Ed.). *The sixth mental measurements yearbook.* Highland Park, New Jersey: Gryphon Press, 1965.

Buser, R. L., & Miller, H. G. *An evaluation instrument for adult and continuing education centers and programs.* Carbondale, Illinois: Southern Illinois University, College of Education, 1973. (ERIC Document Reproduction Service No. ED 064 591)

DeCecco, J. P. *The psychology of learning and instruction: Educational psychology.* Englewood Cliffs, New Jersey: Prentice-Hall, 1968.

Diederich, P. *Shortcut statistics for teacher-made tests.* Princeton, New Jersey: Educational Testing Service, 1960.

Evaluation. Englewood Cliffs, New Jersey: Prentice-Hall, 1973.

Gronlund, N. E. *Measurement and evaluation in teaching.* New York: Macmillan Co., 1965.

Grotelueschen, A. D., Gooler, D. D., Knox, A. B., Kemmis, S., Dowdy, I., & Brophy, K. *An evaluation planner.* Urbana: University of Illinois, 1974.

Hills, J. R. *Measurement and evaluation in the classroom.* Columbus: Charles E. Merrill Publishing Co., 1976.

Miller, H. G. School practice and philosophy: Are they congruent? *Kappa Delta Pi Record.* In press.

National Association for Public Continuing and Adult Education. *You can be a successful teacher of adults.* Washington, D.C.: Author, 1974.

Payne, D. A. *The specification and measurement of learning outcomes.* Waltham, Mass.: Blaisdell Publishing Co., 1968.

Tyler, R. W. General statement on evaluation. *Journal of Educational Research,* 1942, *35* (7), 492-501.

Williams, R., & Miller, H. G. Grading students: A failure to communicate. *The Clearing House,* 1973, *47* (6), 332-337.

10

Community Services and Instruction

Some of the richest sources of information, materials, and learning experiences for any instructional program are community service programs and agencies. For many years the public schools have made use of the varied instructional resources of the community. Adult educators would do well to borrow the idea of community resource utilization from the schools. Far too little attention has been given to the valuable instructional assistance which is available in every community.

The adult performance level concept recognizes the importance of providing the adult with those skills most needed to cope with the problems of modern society. There is general agreement among adult educators that adults who best overcome their problems are those who know where to turn when in need. In recent years community agencies have placed priority on publicizing their services and informing community residents about available programs. Many communities have available a directory of community services compiled by a community services council, a local public welfare or health department, or the public library. The general purpose of these directories has been to provide information on sources of help in such areas as health and welfa employment, housing, consumer affairs, personal problems, a local government. Most have been published for and distributed low income/low educational attainment persons or families.

COMMUNITY SERVICES DIRECTORY

The adult educator should first determine whether a local community services directory is available and which agency or agencies have compiled it. The existing community services directory will be useful to individual adult students with information needs, to the adult teacher in counseling individual students, and to the adult teacher in designing classroom experiences using community resources. This directory will often be compiled by such agencies as the chamber of commerce, one major social agency, a combination of social agencies, or perhaps a larger adult education center.

Content of the Directory

The directory is basically a list of community agencies and a subject index of the different types of services available in the community. The directory will include a general statement of purpose, a discussion of the intended target groups, an indication of sponsorship, and a description of the geographic area included. Most of the following agencies will be included depending on the availability of these services in each locality:

    1.0 *Agencies with area-wide significance*
        1.1 Public library
        1.2 Development council
    2.0 *Community service center*—If one exists it can be of invaluable assistance in directing citizens to the agencies listed in the directory.

3.0 *Emergency phone numbers*
    3.1 Ambulance services if publicly operated
    3.2 Fire—for all communities in the region
    3.3 Police—for all communities in the region
4.0 *Public officials—county and city*
    4.1 County commissioners
    4.2 State's attorney
    4.3 County clerk
    4.4 Circuit clerk
    4.5 Treasurer
    4.6 Assessor
    4.7 Sheriff
    4.8 Superintendent of schools
    4.9 Coroner
    4.10 Circuit judge
    4.11 Superintendent of highways
    4.12 City clerk
    4.13 City mayor
    4.14 City commissioners
5.0 *Directory of schools*—names of schools and school officials
6.0 *Social service agencies*
    6.1 Alcoholics Anonymous
    6.2 County General Assistance Office
    6.3 County Housing Authority
    6.4 American Red Cross
    6.5 Cooperative University Extension Service
    6.6 Chamber of Commerce
    6.7 Adult Schools
    6.8 Community Centers
    6.9 Division of Unemployment Compensation
    6.10 Farmers Home Administration
    6.11 Homemakers Program
    6.12 Department of Children and Family Services
    6.13 Department of Mental Health or Community Mental Health Center

6.14 Department of Public Welfare
6.15 Migrant Council
6.16 State Employment Service
6.17 Veterans' Administration
6.18 Legal Assistance
6.19 Licensed Day Care Centers (public)
6.20 Youth Centers
6.21 Long-Term Care Units
6.22 Recreation Centers
6.23 Senior Citizens' Centers
6.24 Nutritional Centers
6.25 Social Security Administration
6.26 Tuberculosis and Respiratory Disease Association
6.27 Driver's License Examination Stations
6.28 County Health Department
6.29 Public Health Clinics

The directory will contain the following information about each of the agencies listed: (1) official agency name, (2) director's name, (3) address, (4) phone number, (5) groups served, and (6) services each agency provides. Sample entries in the directory might look something like the following:

HEALTH AND WELFARE RESOURCES

Alcoholics Anonymous
  Wilbur Watts, Director
  202 Gaslight Avenue
  George, IL 00728
  Phone: 212-8468

Groups served: People with alcohol or alcohol-related problems.

Services: Some of the agency's services include a temporary home for sober alcoholics, room and board, basic education and job training, hospital care, help in finding jobs, counseling and educational programs on alcoholism. A brochure is available upon request.

Herrmann County Adult Education Center
Duff Jones, Director
5116 Apple Street
George, IL 00728
Phone: 212-4616

Groups served: Any adult in need of training or education to complete a high school equivalency program.

Services: Educational classes are offered in the following areas: GED (General Educational Development), Basic Education, Auto Mechanics, Welding, Carpentry Woodworking, Cabinetmaking, Electricity, Printing, Shorthand, Typing, Nurse's Aide, Upholstery, First Aid, Income Tax Preparation, Metric System, Speech, Driver Education.

State Department of Children and Family Services
1519 Tree Street
George, IL 00728
Phone: 212-2111

Groups served: Families with children under eighteen, where such services are not otherwise provided by other public or voluntary agencies.

Services: Basic services are in the following eight areas: (1) protective services for the abused, (2) investigation of claims of the abused, (3) foster care, (4) services for unmarried mothers, (5) adoption services, (6) licensing services, (7) family counseling, and (8) day care services.

Preparation of the Directory

Regardless of the sponsoring agency, adult educators and students can become involved in various phases of the planning, preparation, updating, promotion, or distribution of the community services directory. The compilation of a comprehensive directory is a large undertaking—one that needs adequate agency resources for completion—but adult students can learn much about available community services by assisting in this effort. If the community already has a social services directory, the adult class could become involved in updating the existing information or in distributing additional copies in their neighborhoods. If no such directory exists, the adult education class might want to propose to the appropriate agencies that such a project be undertaken. Adult students could be included on the planning committee.

In order for interested adult teachers and adult students to know how to participate effectively in various phases of the preparation of the community services directory, the following basic steps in the preparation or updating of the directory are described:

1. Identify the sponsoring agency and organize a planning committee. Adult teachers and adult students can be members of this committee, along with representatives of other social agencies and community groups.
2. Identify community agencies to be included in the directory, and prepare interview forms to be used with the agencies.
3. Organize interview teams of agency workers, community workers, adult students, school personnel, and other interested volunteers. These teams will schedule interviews with specific agencies and will receive training in interview techniques and in the use of the specific interview forms.
4. Conduct personal interviews with agency personnel, rather than by mail or by phone. It is important that data be complete and readable.
5. Promote the project through the news media.
6. Edit the entries for each community group and return the edited copy to the person interviewed in each agency as a check for omitted or erroneous information.
7. Print copies of the directory in an attractive and easy-to-use format.

8. Distribute the directory, paying particular attention to those identified as target groups. Adult classes and public agencies having direct contact with the underemployed and the undereducated are useful distribution points.
9. Establish a plan for updating and reissue.

USING THE DIRECTORY IN THE CLASSROOM

The adult instructor can use community resources identified in the social services directory to enhance the adult student's life coping skills and to involve community agency personnel in the adult education program. The teacher can prepare the adult students for classroom presentations by community workers in a number of ways.

1. Students can consider the role of helping agencies within the community. Students may report briefly about some occasion when they have benefited by the efforts of one of the agencies listed in the directory. For a writing exercise, the students could compose and read to the class a paper in which they try to imagine a society with no helping agencies. The teacher can point out that this is not too unrealistic, since most of these agencies have existed for only a short time.
2. The class can discuss a specific agency, and one or more students can role play the position of the agency director.
3. The students list the agencies which they are interested in and develop questions about these agencies. The adult instructor must be careful not to perform this task for his or her students; if this occurs, the objectives or goals will be the teacher's and not the students'.
4. Using their questions the students draw up a format which representatives of the agencies will follow. (It is important that the students understand that not all invited speakers will follow this suggested format.)

5. Each student rank orders the agencies about which he or she would like more information. (The students should exclude the community service center since it will logically be the first agency studied.)
6. A student committee can be formed to draw up a composite rank ordering. (The teacher should point out that it may be necessary to deviate from the composite order if one agency's presentation naturally leads to information about another agency.)

Students will now be ready to learn about helping agencies. At the same time through a variety of teaching methods they can improve their reading, writing, arithmetic, and other academic skills. Adult teachers in all types of adult classes are urged to seek uses for the vast wealth of resources which exist in every community and to use the helping agencies as a beginning to identify those resources. Some useful methods of instruction follow.

Presentation Method #1—Lecture

Mentioned first, because it is the method of presentation with which most agency representatives will feel comfortable, is the lecture or factual speech. Without question, this is the easiest presentation method for the average speaker. The presenter identifies his agency and the contact persons within the agency, describes the agency's functions or services, explains procedures for obtaining services, and outlines restrictions upon the agency. Normally interaction occurs if at all only during a question and answer session. The experienced adult teacher will recognize that while this may be a reasonably comfortable approach for the speaker, it is not highly productive for the listener. Since it is unlikely that most invited agency speakers will be prepared to vary from the standard lecture format, the teacher should make an effort to arrange for that needed variety. One suggestion is to incorporate the presentation with a coffee. This will provide an informal atmosphere and may relax the speaker and the audience. Adult students can prepare questions in advance for the speaker.

For best results, the speaker should be introduced by a student, and a student should serve as moderator for the session. It is not unreasonable to suggest to the speaker that any audiovisual materials that he may have would make his presentation more successful. The speaker should also be encouraged to distribute informational pamphlets if available.

Presentation Method #2—Agency Panel

This method is useful when the agencies making up the panel provide similar or related services or in some way function in conjunction with each other. The major value of this method is its ability to demonstrate the relationships among many agencies. Additionally, the presence of more than one presenter suggests that the topic is important and provides variety. This type of presentation requires coordination and preplanning, especially if duplication is to be avoided. Unfortunately, this becomes its major weakness, since far too little planning is normally undertaken by those making panel presentations.

Presentation Method #3—Interview

The success of the interview method for presenting an agency or service depends on the level of pre-interview preparation on the part of the interviewer. Generally speaking, it is expected that the interviewer will need to be knowledgeable about the agency in question. Furthermore, interviewing is a rather high level skill. Unless the interview is performed skillfully, it will move slowly and could prove to be an unsatisfactory method of presentation. It would undoubtedly be beneficial to have those who are going to conduct the interview spend some time practicing the necessary techniques, especially reflecting the responses of the person being interviewed and picking up on clues leading to additional points. If the interviewer is skillful, this presentation method has the advantage of helping the nervous presenter make a coherent presentation. It also provides the students with the opportunity to discover what constitutes an adequate interview. Even when this technique is utilized, opportunity should be provided for those who wish to ask questions concerning areas which they feel require further clarification.

Presentation Method #4—Agency Visit

In this instance, part or all of the class is given an opportunity to observe the agency in actual or simulated operation. Since most public agencies would be unwilling to conduct demonstrations using actual clients, members of the class can act as clients and follow the procedures of the agency as a regular client would. The utilization of this method requires that the agency is active at night or is willing to be, or that the class is able to adjust its schedule to meet the time requirements of the agency. For best results a large group should be split into smaller groups; several stations can be set up where activities may be demonstrated. One of the great advantages of this method is that familiarity with the agency office and its operation may reduce the fear class members have in making use of the agency and its services.

Presentation Method #5—Agency Game

One method of presenting an agency is the game or simulation. With this plan various members of the class act as agency representatives, and other class members are clients. An adequate presentation requires that each member of the presenting group understands his or her role well. An agency representative should brief the class on agency services and procedures and should be present to point out flaws or errors in the presentation. This technique requires extensive preparation, but it encourages participation and involvement to a greater extent than other presentation methods. It is also possible to use the agency game to examine for a second time agencies which have already been discussed, either to review the services of significant agencies (such as an employment agency) or to provide an opportunity for students to be involved in the technique itself.

Presentation Method #6—Radio Program or Play

Three methods should be considered in using the radio to provide variety in the presentation of service agencies. First, an actual radio interview may be arranged and presented. Public service time may be obtained for such purposes, and no charges should be incurred. For the live broadcast, an agency representative plus a member of the class should be included in the activity. An interview format might be used to advantage, or the program could include a general statement by the student as to why he or she is interested in learning about the agency, followed by a general statement by the agency representative. In some instances, a better program may be produced by the second method of prerecording the program for later broadcast. The obvious advantage is that the material may be edited to eliminate errors and to keep the program within time constraints. The third method is the broadcast simulation. This may be accomplished either by having students act as though they were making a live radio broadcast which is tape recorded so the participants may later review the program or by having a microphone connected to a radio for amplification. The first two methods have the advantage of being received by persons other than class members and thereby providing both additional agency coverage and educational program publicity.

Presentation Method #7—Audiovisual Production

Variety may be provided and interest enhanced through student-produced audiovisual presentations about particular agencies. These may take the form of 8mm films, slide-tape presentations, videotapes, and audiotapes. Students should plan the presentation, do the actual production work, and write the script. Slide-tape presentations are particularly easy to produce, equipment is readily available and easy to use, production costs are low, and the finished product can be edited and updated readily. Videotape may be used for recording agency operations, as well as presentations made by agency personnel in the classroom. Videotape recording equipment can usually be borrowed through the public school system or the local community college. Occasionally, it may be necessary and even desirable to have an agency make its presentation through the use of audiotape. Certainly this is not the best method and should be used only as a last resort when no other more personal method is available. It is also good to audiotape all speakers who appear before the group so that students who are absent may at least hear the presentation.

Presentation Method #8—Community Leaders

With this method, community leaders are asked to come into the classroom to discuss the total area of community services. The principle advantage is that both the adult students and the leaders of the community are made aware of the strengths and weaknesses of the services which the community provides to its citizens. Additionally, this is another method by which the citizens of the community may be made aware of adult education and the need for lifelong learning.

Presentation Method #9—Class Evaluation of Agencies and Their Functions

Evaluation assumes knowledge and thoughtful application of that knowledge. No discussion or study of agencies should conclude without a thorough evaluation of each agency individually and agencies collectively. Evaluation requires student involvement in the recall and utilization of what has been learned.

SELECTED BIBLIOGRAPHY

Ashley, M., & Norsworth, G. F. *Facilitating learning through the use of supportive services in Adult Basic Education.* Tallahassee, Florida: Florida State University, Department of Adult Education, 1971.

Childers, T. *The information-poor in America.* Metuchen, New Jersey: Scarecrow Press, 1975.

Community resources and supportive services—Lesson 24. In *Basic education: Teaching the adult—Teacher education series.* Baltimore: Maryland State Department of Education, Division of Instructional Television, 1975. (30-minute videotape and lesson plan)

Croneburger, R., Kapechky, M., & Luck, C. *The library as a community information and referral center.* Morehead, Kentucky: Morehead State University, Appalachian Adult Education Center, 1975. (ERIC Document Reproduction Service No. ED 108 653)

Donahue, J. D., & Kochen, M. *Information for the community.* Chicago: American Library Association, 1976.

Identifying community resources—Package No. 6. In *SAGE (Skills for Adult Guidance Educators) handbook.* Portland, Oregon: Northwest Regional Educational Laboratory, 1975.

Information and referral services series. Minneapolis, Minnesota: American Rehabilitation Foundation, 1971.
Titles in the series are:
A training syllabus (ERIC Document Reproduction Service No. ED 055 632)
Notes for managers (ERIC Document Reproduction Service No. ED 055 633)
The resource file (ERIC Document Reproduction Service No. ED 055 634)
Interviewing and information giving (ERIC Document Reproduction Service No. ED 055 635)
Referral procedures (ERIC Document Reproduction Service No. ED 055 636)
Follow up (ERIC Document Reproduction Service No. ED 055 637)
Volunteer escort service (ERIC Document Reproduction Service No. ED 055 638)
The role of advocacy (ERIC Document Reproduction Service No. ED 055 639)
Reaching out (ERIC Document Reproduction Service No. ED 055 640)

Ogg, E. *Tell me where to turn; the growth of information and referral services.* New York: Public Affairs Publications, 1971. (Pamphlet and 16mm film)

11

Competency-Based Instruction for Adults

Throughout much of this volume concern has been expressed for the performance of the adult student as he moves through some instructional activity. The kinds of behavior displayed at the end of instruction are the important factors to consider. Performance, behavioral objectives, and competency have been stressed in the instructional process. This emphasis on behavior and the competency of students after instruction is consistent with the position now being advocated by researchers and practitioners in many different fields of education. In fact considerable curriculum development work based on competency models is occurring in secondary education, teacher education, administrative education, and adult education. The impetus for developing a comprehensive competency-based curriculum in adult education is largely the result of the findings of the Adult Performance Level (APL) Study conducted at the University of Texas (Northcutt, 1975).

In the extensive APL Study, five adult needs or general knowledge areas were identified and defined. The areas—Consumer Economics, Occupational Knowledge, Community Resources, Health, and Government and Law—are the important content areas of adult literacy and adult performance in society. Besides these critical general knowledge areas, four primary skills were also identified. These primary skills—Communication, Computation, Problem Solving and Interpersonal Relations—account for the vast majority of requirements placed on adults in society. The APL Study has thus defined the content and skill areas important to undereducated adults and has begun to integrate them through curriculum development work in competency areas.

In the curriculum development process one of the general knowledge areas is identified, and competency requirements are described for it in three successive levels of detail. The first level is the goal statement level. This is a broad description of the capability that the functionally competent adult should possess. the particular general knowledge area.

The goal statement is then defined more precisely by a series of intermediate-level requirements called objectives. The objective is perceived as the basic building block of the APL description of competency. Some degree of mastery of these objectives, depending on the student's individual milieu, is required for true functional competency.

Each objective is described by a series of situation-specific requirements called tasks. Mastery of the objective is thus demonstrated by the student's ability to perform a group of tasks or to respond appropriately to specific situations which meet the requirements of the objective. The ability to perform tasks indicates the mastery of the objective. The mastery of several appropriate objectives indicates that the goal statement has been fulfilled.

This APL Study focuses on basic education and literacy training for the undereducated adult and, of course, is not representative of all adult and continuing education instructional efforts. It does, however, focus on the use and potential strength of competency-based adult instruction in terms of what adult students can do after some instruction has occurred. The flexibility of the basic APL idea is notable, and numerous modifications have been made both locally and statewide in the Adult Basic Education area (Parker, 1976). More undoubtedly will follow.

This trend toward more competency-based instruction will continue in the field of adult education. In fact, competency-based ideas are likely to replace eighth grade level or high school level equivalency standards as common barometers of achievement. With this movement underway it might be well to conclude this volume on adult instruction with a review of some strengths and possible shortcomings in the area of competency-based instruction for adults.

The word *competency* in most of the recent literature indicates an emphasis on "the ability to do" as opposed to a more traditional emphasis on "the ability to demonstrate knowledge." The newer idea suggests that the adult student can perform the given behavior in overt terms upon completion of instuction. The new behavior is performed and not merely stored in knowledge form. Even though "performance" is generally seen as part of "competency," the two terms are generally viewed as synonymous. Competencies are viewed as knowledge, skills, and behaviors in any field of endeavor, whether cognitive, psychomotor, or affective.

STRENGTHS

Competency-based instructional advocates suggest that its major strength is that it is learner oriented. In competency-based programming the emphasis shifts from the teacher and the teaching process to the learner and the learning process. It is individualized; the learners can proceed at their own pace. These qualities are important for the adult learner.

Performance- or competency-based programs offer explicit and precise learning goals or objectives. The goals specify exactly what is to be achieved and the standards of performance that will be acceptable; the learner knows exactly what is expected of him or her. Because of these standards of performance or assessment criteria, there are strong measures of accountability built into these programs. With clear, precise goals and the criteria specified to measure performance, the adult student has before him just what is expected from the learning experience (objective) and the means to check to see if he did in fact achieve what he set out to do (assessment criteria). Inherent in this type of instructional programming is the concept of immediate feedback. The adult learner under the guidance of his instructor can immediately ascertain his degree of accomplishment and determine what if anything further needs to be done. Finally, in the area of measurement the process is criterion-referenced and not norm-referenced. In this case the learning is measured against some previously specified criteria designed for the individual adult learner and not against some standardized norm or against a whole class of students.

Competency-based material can be very pragmatic for adults because it can focus directly on the important concerns of society and the needs of adults to function adequately in society. Community information can be used as an important resource in the learning process. Further, competency-based instruction actually stresses exit requirements rather than entrance requirements and permits the learner to go at his own pace and to repeat, if necessary, experiences or tasks until mastery is achieved. Because of the emphasis on exit rather than entrance requirements, competency-based instruction can encourage adults of every age to enter the educational stream to continue their personal and professional growth and even to prepare for new careers.

There are several considerations that should be brought to the attention of adult instructors when they begin developmental work in competency-based instruction. First, the entire process should be broadly based in terms of the decision-making process. Adult student involvement is critical to the success of a learning program. Students, instructors, and others should participate in specifying goals and developing assessment criteria. Adult students and instructors can design learning experiences based on agreed-upon goals. The learning experiences and tasks should include as much hands-on, field-oriented activity as possible. This brings more personal meaning to the experience and gives direct perceptual intake to the adult learner. Greater flexibility is also required in programming because competency-based instruction runs counter to the more traditional credit hour and course and classroom arrangements. Well designed and carefully selected materials are important to gaining the behaviors specified; the learning experiences should contribute directly to the accomplishment of the tasks. Finally, in competency-based instruction there should be immediate feedback to the adult learner as he proceeds through the experience. Awareness of progress throughout a learning experience is critical to the adult learner.

POTENTIAL SHORTCOMINGS

One major concern expressed is that this type of instructional programming can be a very mechanical, inflexible, assembly-line process. The adult student can be required to move from Task A to Task B to Task C in learning a new behavior or competency. This process can be very rigid, and it can stifle interest if the teacher is not careful. The adult instructor should see that there is variety in the tasks and experiences given to adult students and that ample opportunity is afforded to the students to interact with instructors and fellow students during the learning process. Personal interaction, variety, and continuous feedback can reduce the mechanical nature of competency-based instruction.

A second concern, which relates closely to the first, is that this type of instructional programming can fragment the curriculum or the subject matter. In fact, the sum of the parts may not equal the whole major concept or principle under consideration. Caution must be exercised by the instructor to assure that all parts or individual behaviors are related and that total meaning is derived by the adult learner. Learning isolated competencies without understanding how to apply them will do little to enhance the adult learner's total behavior. A total conceptualization of the program is required for it to be effective.

A third concern is that competency-based instruction inhibits creative effort on the part of the adult learner. This need not be the case in many learning experiences. Granted there cannot be much creative effort or expression for the adult student when he or she is adding two-digit numbers in a basic math class or when the adult is learning to spell certain words. In other areas, however, the adult student can be asked to use creative abilities and to apply what is learned to a variety of situations. Adult students can develop alternative solutions to existing problems; suggest different ways of doing things; design or create new objects, techniques, or strategies; or deal with problems and concerns in the student's own world. Creative tasks can be built into the adult learner's experiences if the adult instructor feels that it is important.

A final major concern is that performance- or competency-based instruction is nonhumanistic and lacks concern for the student. There could be a tendency to teach adults only cognitive knowledge and psychomotor skills and techniques and to ignore the affective area. An adult student, therefore, may be skilled in welding, sewing, or construction; but he may have little feel for the process, his world, his fellowman, or himself. This could easily happen if little or no concern is shown for the adult learner, his goals, values, and ideas. The key to overcoming this major problem is, of course, involvement with and for the adult learner. The instructor must work with the learner at every point in the process, from goal definition to assessment of outcomes, and relate carefully to the learner during the entire procedure. The individualized nature of the instructional process will assist the teacher in this effort.

It is hoped that the discussion of the strengths and possible shortcomings of competency-based instruction will assist the adult educator in designing more effective instructional programs.

Developmental activities, occurring in a variety of areas, have resulted from a careful analysis of the needs and goals of adult learners in their own social milieu. Numerous alternatives are available in Adult Basic Education, but competency-based instruction can be developed in all other areas of adult education, such as vocational education, continuing education, and enrichment. Creative thinking and implementation by adult educators, working in conjunction with their students, can provide appropriate learning experiences for all adult students.

SELECTED BIBLIOGRAPHY

Mulvey, M. C. (Ed.). *Adult performance level related educational products developed by Section 309 Special Projects.* Washington, D.C.: Government Printing Office, 1975.

Northcutt, N. *Adult functional competency: A summary.* Austin, Texas: University of Texas at Austin, Division of Extension, 1975.

Parker, J. (Ed.). *Competency-based adult education research and innovation catalog.* Washington, D.C.: Government Printing Office, 1976.

INDEX

Adult behavior
  affective, 17, 58-59
  bases of, 10-11
  cognitive, 16, 56-58
  domains of, 16-17, 56-61
  nature of, 9-15
  needs affecting, 12-13
  psychomotor, 17, 60-61
Adult education. *See also*
    Instruction of adults
  history of, 36-39
  improvement of, 5-6
  institutions involved in, 2-4
  legislation, 40-45
  need for, 1-2
  philosophy of, 35-36
  political forces, 28-30, 40-45
Adult educators, 4-5
Adult instruction. *See* Instruction
    of adults
Adult Performance Level
    Survey, 192
Adults as learners, 9-16
Affective behavior, 17, 58-59
Anecdotal records, 171-172
APL Study, 192
Assessment techniques. *See*
    Evaluation; Post testing;
    Pretesting; Tests
Assignments. *See also* Puzzles
  checklist for, 89-90
  types of, 102-120

Behavior
  three domains of, 16-17, 56-61
Behavioral objectives, 73-78, 82.
    See also Objectives
  advantages & disadvantages, 73-74
  examples of, 74-78
  how to write, 74-78
Brainstorming group, 146

Checklists, use in testing, 166-168
Classroom climate, 63-64, 121
Cognitive behavior, 16, 56-58

Community resources, classroom
    use of, 177-178
Community services directory
  classroom use, 183-188
  content of, 178-181
  preparation of, 181-183
Competency-based instruction,
    191-197
  advantages of, 193-195
  disadvantages of, 195-197
Completion tests, 163-164
Content organization, types of,
    84-89
Curriculum design, 21-31
Curriculum model, 31

Demonstrations, 128-130
Discussion groups, 147
Drill, 135-139
Drill exercises, 136-139

Essay tests, 164-165
Evaluations. *See also* Pretesting;
    Post testing; Tests
  of courses, 157-158
  in curriculum process, 24-26
  formative, 26
  levels of, 155-158
  of programs, 155-157
  summative, 26
  uses of, 153-155
Evaluation techniques. *See* Post
    testing; Pretesting; Tests
Explanation, 126-128

Goals, 22-23, 68-71. *See also*
    Objectives
Groups, in instruction, 145-149

Inquiry process, 143-145
Instruction of adults
  competency-based, 191-197
  content organization, 84-89
  future directions of, 191-197
  general strategies for, 12-16,
    63-64, 91-92, 121

individualized, 15
methods for, 125-149, 183-188
model of, 49-51
psychological implications, 12-16
use of community resources in,
   177-188
Instructional design, 49-51. *See also*
   Instruction of adults
Instructional plans, 81-93
Instructional techniques, 125-149,
   183-188. *See also under specific
   techniques* and Instruction of
   adults

Learning activities. *See also* Puzzles
checklist for, 89-90
types of, 102-120
Learning theory, adult, 9-15
Lecture, 126-128
Legislation, 40-45
Lesson plans
   component parts, 81-90
   examples of, 93-102
   organization of, 81-93
   uses of, 82

Maslow, Abraham, 12-13
Matching tests, 160-162
Multiple-choice tests, 159-160

Needs, hierarchy of, 12-13

Objective tests, types of, 158-164
Objectives, 52-61, 67-78. *See also*
   Behavioral objectives
levels of, 68-71
purposes of, 67-68
selection of, 71-73
taxonomies of, 16-17, 56-61
types of, 54-56

Performance-based education. *See*
   Competency-based education
Performance tests, types of, 165-172
Political forces, 28-30, 40-45
Post testing, 64, 90-91. *See also* Tests;
   Evaluation

Pretesting, 52-53, 83
Program evaluation, 155-157
Psychology of adult behavior, 9-15
Psychomotor behavior, 17, 60-61
Puzzles
   crossword, 102-104
   cryptogram, 110-111
   missing letter search, 111-113
   word scramble, 108-109
   wordsearch, 105-107

Questioning techniques, 130-135

Rating scales, 168-171

Skill learning, 60-61
   evaluation of, 165-172
Small groups, 145-149
Social agencies, use of, in classroom,
   183-188
Standardized tests, 158
Student evaluation. *See* Evaluation;
   Post testing; Pretesting; Tests

Teachers of adults, 4-5
Teaching methods, 125-149, 183-188.
   See also under specific techniques
   and Instruction of adults
Tests, 158-174
   completion, 163-164
   criterion-referenced, 25-26, 173-174
   essay, 164-165
   matching, 160-162
   multiple-choice, 159-160
   norm-referenced, 25, 173
   objective, 158-164
   performance, 165-172
   standardized, 158
   teacher-made, 158-174
   true-false, 162-163
True-false tests, 162-163
Tutoring, 139-142
   in groups, 148

University of Texas Adult
   Performance Level Study, 192

Dr. John R. Verduin, Jr., has spent fifteen years as a university teacher and administrator of teacher education and adult education programs. He has served as a consultant to the Adult and Continuing Education Section of the Illinois Office of Education. Dr. Verduin is currently professor of educational leadership and co-director of the Southern Illinois Adult Education Service Center at Southern Illinois University at Carbondale.

Dr. Harry Miller is Chairman of the Department of Educational Leadership and Coordinator of the Studies in Adult Education Program at Southern Illinois University at Carbondale. He has published extensively and is currently serving on the editorial board of *Training: Magazine of Human Resources Development.* Dr. Miller has been listed in such biographical works as *Outstanding Educators of America, Leaders in Education,* and *Who's Who in America.*

Mr. Charles Greer has been a full-time adult educator for the past ten of his twenty-six years in public education. His previous experience has included classroom teaching, counseling, and administration. As an adult educator, he directed a nine-county Adult Education Day Center. Currently, Mr. Greer is assistant director of the Southern Illinois Adult Education Service Center at Southern Illinois University at Carbondale.